TOUCHING THE EARTH

Akuppa

TOUCHING THE EARTH

A Buddhist Guide to Saving the Planet

WINDHORSE PUBLICATIONS

Published by Windhorse Publications
11 Park Road
Birmingham
B13 8AB
email: windhorse@compuserve.com
web: www.windhorsepublications.com

Cover design by Marlene Eltschig
Cover photo © Corbis Stock Market
Printed by Biddles Ltd, Guildford, Surrey
Printed on paper from renewable sources

British Library Cataloguing in Publication Data:
A catalogue record for this book is available from the British Library

ISBN   1 899579 48 6

CONTENTS

ABOUT THE AUTHOR

Akuppa, also known as John Wigham, was born in 1962 in Cullercoats, England. After graduating from the University of Oxford with a degree in geography he went on to study for a degree in town planning at the University of Liverpool. He then began a career in local government in Manchester before moving back to the north-east. During his eleven years as a town planner he specialized in environmental matters and worked on Local Agenda 21 issues in Sunderland.

At the same time, Akuppa explored environmental issues in the political sphere. In the late 1980s he campaigned for environmental issues within the Labour movement on Tyneside and later went on to become a Labour councillor in Newcastle upon Tyne for one of the poorest neighbourhoods in the country. He fought strongly to save Newcastle's green belt and a city centre park, and argued against new road proposals. His views often brought him into conflict with the local Labour establishment.

After five years as a councillor he left party politics to devote more of his time to Buddhism. He has increasingly come to see the value of Buddhism in offering the prospect of a fundamental change of values that he found was missing from the political and professional approaches.

In 2000 Akuppa was ordained within the Western Buddhist Order, and given his Buddhist name, which means 'unshakeable'. He is currently based at Newcastle Buddhist Centre and teaches meditation and Buddhism in schools, universities, and prisons.

ACKNOWLEDGEMENTS

My warm thanks to those people who have commented on successive drafts of this book and helped to make it very much better than it would otherwise have been, namely Jnanasiddhi, Subhadassi, and Ratnaprabha. Thanks to the team at Windhorse Publications for their help and encouragement. For general stimulation and inspiration in helping me think about Buddhism and the environment, I'm particularly grateful to Saramati and Lokabandhu. And I am most grateful to my teacher, Urgyen Sangharakshita, whose contribution to this book is so overarching that I almost forgot to thank him.

Thanks also to Pauline and John Pearson, who very generously gave me the use of Farne Cottage, where I hid away to write the first draft. For other practical acts of kindness while I was writing, thanks to David Cornwell, Darshan, Toby Smith, and my parents, Arthur and Betty Wigham. Finally, thanks to my housemates for their general forbearance while I was absorbed in the task.

FOR HEROIC SPIRITS INTENDED

It was some nine years ago that I seriously began to practise the teachings of the Buddha. I already had a long-standing personal interest in environmental issues and had been engaged in them through my work as a town planner and involvement in local politics. It was clear to me from the outset that there was some affinity between Buddhism and environmental concern. Since then, with the help of others, I have reflected on what that affinity is and on how these two areas of my life might fit together. I thought for a time that Buddhism might need to be changed to accommodate modern environmental concern. More and more, however, I have come to be convinced that the essence of the Buddha's teachings is timeless. The path of transformation they offer is of immense value to the environmental movement, and, indeed, to any human being in the modern world. It also seems to me that some regard for the environmental predicament is a natural and even indispensable part of being a Buddhist. In this book, I explore this valuable treasure that Buddhism has to offer environmentalism, as well as the importance to the Buddhist of an environmental perspective.

First, though, an echo of a warning originally used as a preface to an ancient Buddhist sutra.[1] This book is 'for heroic spirits intended'. Buddhism is not just another intellectual, political, or even religious position. Nor is it to be plundered as a source of bland homilies about compassion or the nature of the universe. Its true value lies in the practical path of transformation that it offers, both for us and for the world. To test this, you will need to engage your heart as well as your mind. It is for such heroic spirits that this book is intended.

But there is a more particular reason why a certain heroism of spirit might be needed in reading this book; particularly the next chapter, which deals with the environmental crisis itself. I have to confess that, when I hear a radio programme or see a magazine article about the destruction of the Amazonian rainforest, my immediate reaction is to want to switch channels or turn the page. It's not that I don't care about the rainforest. It's just that the inevitable statistics about the rate of its disappearance (often measured in pieces of land the size of Wales) are simply too depressing. I already know about the issue, I don't buy tropical hardwoods, and there seems to be little else I can do about it. What could I, as one person, possibly do that would make anything more than the most minute difference? Why just make myself miserable?

Such feelings of despair and powerlessness are common reactions to global environmental problems. The complex of conditions that bring them about seems too vast and too distant to exert any influence over whatsoever. This can result in a kind of alienated fatalism: we carry on with our lives, but with a dull sense of anxiety and pessimism about the future.

We can always choose to listen only to the more reassuring experts or, indeed, not to listen to any at all. Messengers of doomsday are not, after all, a new thing, but, as yet, no all-consuming apocalypse has overtaken us. Those of us without the benefit of several scientific degrees have to rely on the say-so of experts to judge the nature and extent of the environmental crisis. This can be a bewildering experience. Scientists often disagree about the facts, or they agree about the facts but come up with different interpretations of them. Almost weekly we read of new research findings and new predictions, sometimes alarming, sometimes reassuring, but a substantial majority of scientific opinion is pointing out the catastrophic and irreversible consequences of our actions. Even if the thousands of scientists working for respected organizations such as the Intergovernmental Panel on Climate Change and the World Conservation Union might be getting it wrong, the stakes are so high that it would be foolish not to take them seriously. If we waited until the evidence was completely incontrovertible, it would be too late to do anything about it anyway. We can deny the evidence, or we can acknowledge that it matters.

The desire to continue with business as usual, to avoid any implications we don't like, can be very strong. If you think you may have exceeded your overdraft limit, you might be tempted not to open your bank statements, believing, somewhere in the back of your mind, that this will make the problem go away. It doesn't work, I have found, yet this is exactly how we as a society behave with regard to some environmental issues.

Despair or denial is not an unnatural response to the situation; it is even understandable. But, somehow, we need to get to the point where we can face up to the problems, work out the implications, and act accordingly. To do this, we need to acknowledge any despair we feel and move on. We need to take a cool, objective look at the evidence.

If we are stuck in negative feelings such as despair and alienation, we are likely to overlook the very thing that can help us move on. The fact that we have felt despair in the first place indicates that we must have at least some spark of concern about other people, about future generations, about animals, or about the beauty of nature. It is this capacity to look beyond ourselves that makes a truly human existence possible. This seed of heroism is the most precious part of being human. In the Buddhist view, it is a seed that can be cultivated and grown. If we do look beyond ourselves, we might be surprised to find that – in a thousand ordinary ways – real change is possible after all.

two

THE AWAKENING HEART AND MIND

Imagine you are sitting on one of the Pacific islands of Tuvalu. Opposite you is a woman called Tubwebwe.[2] As you talk, she is patiently straining the juice of a nonu fruit to produce a remedy for breathing difficulties – a cure that has been handed down the generations. She enjoys life on the island, surrounded by family and friends in a traditional society that makes its living from the sea. As she looks over to her three children playing nearby, her smiling face is clouded by an expression of anxiety. She has been told that the sea is rising and that within a generation or two the islands may disappear. What will become of her home, her children, her friends' children? What will become of their way of life?

Imagine you are in a crowded slum area of Dhaka, Bangladesh, talking with a twenty-year-old woman called Honufa.[3] She talks about the conditions in which she lives: 'Every day there is disease in this slum; diarrhoea, dysentery, stomach pains, and headaches. Children suffer the most. Everything is packed into a tiny space here, you can imagine the unhealthy situation we live in. I've lost a two-year-old son from a diarrhoeal disease and there are two other women in this room that I know have also lost children to diarrhoea due to the unsanitary conditions here.'

Imagine you are in what remains of the Atlantic Forest of eastern Brazil. Ninety per cent of the forest has already been lost and, in the distance, you can hear the sound of loggers taking more trees for their timber and to make way for new roads. In the trees, you catch a glance of the face of a monkey surrounded by an exotic halo of golden hair. It is a species of lion tamarin that lives only in that forest, and there are fewer than a thousand left.

We are living in a world of extremes. A small minority of the world's population lives in unprecedented affluence, reaping the fruits of new technology and the increasingly global economy. For a much greater number of people, existence is marginal. In one way or another, they are struggling to cope with rapid changes that are happening all over the world. Cities across Asia, Africa, and Latin America are expanding so rapidly that millions of children are left to fend for themselves on the streets. Pacific islanders face the prospect of losing their homes as sea levels rise. Wild places and their animals and plants are being lost to exploitation and urbanization.

How are we to respond, looking upon this world from the vantage point of a comfortable, affluent society?

Our predicament is not entirely new. Siddhartha Gautama, who would become known as the Buddha, was born about 2,500 years ago to a privileged élite in the emerging urban civilization of the Ganges Basin. His parents were wealthy and powerful and he was brought up with all the wealth, security, and status that his society could offer. He enjoyed a happy childhood inside his parents' palace, but when he grew to be a young man, he became dissatisfied with his lifestyle, feeling hemmed in by assumptions and expectations. One day, while riding through the streets of his home city in his chariot, he was struck by the reality of human suffering. He saw sickness, old age, and death as though for the first time, and realized that no one, rich or poor, could escape them.

The world that we look upon in our day is vastly more complex than the one in which Siddhartha lived. In his time, technology was relatively simple, the scale of human activity relatively small, and the relationship between people and the land still relatively local. Nowadays, not only are there many more people, but the technological energy at our disposal is far greater. Networks of actions and their consequences spread out across the whole world.

It often feels as though we are bombarded with images of suffering. Not only this, but the causes of suffering seem bewildering in their complexity. This can make our temptation to screen ourselves from it all the greater. So to begin with, we have to decide whether or not we really care enough to try to change things. After all, provided that one doesn't pay too much attention to science or nature programmes, or news items about environmental catastrophes, it is still possible – for the time being – to carry on a high-consumption, high-pollution lifestyle. Everyone else, it seems, is still doing it.

A friend of mine was in a department store recently when the fire alarm sounded. Some people started walking calmly towards the exits, others looked to the staff for guidance but found that they were just as uncertain what to do. Many, however, no doubt assuming it was a false alarm, blithely carried on with their shopping. This is the way we all too often behave; rather than take responsibility for our actions, we look to those in authority, or we just go along with what everyone else does. Unless we can see and smell the danger for ourselves, we will tend to carry on as usual. In the world at the moment, the alarm bells are ringing, but the most serious danger is not so much to us, but to future generations and to people in other parts of the world. If we look to those in government, we see indecision or complacency. If we look to those around us, we see many people carrying on as usual. So what do we do? Do we follow the herd, or do we look to our own sense of what is rational and compassionate?

Siddhartha could have put his experience of suffering from his mind and settled back into a comfortable life of privilege. No doubt there were many voices urging him to do so. In the end, though, they did not prevail and Siddhartha decisively left behind all the wealth and security of his position. He embarked on a quest to end suffering – not just the actual suffering he had witnessed while riding around his home city, but all suffering. He wanted to get to the root of suffering, through sickness, old age, and death, or through feeling hemmed in as he had, or through struggling to find a sense of purpose and fulfilment.

Soon after setting out on his quest, Siddhartha swapped his expensive clothes for rags and cut his hair – both would have been a mark of his status. He then went to live in the forest with those who seemed to share his purpose most closely – the holy men, common in India at the time, who had dedicated themselves to meditation and ascetic practices as a way to the truth.

Siddhartha was nothing if not wholehearted. We could try to emulate him quite literally, climate permitting, by taking to the wilderness ourselves. But there are other ways of following in his footsteps. They might not entail wearing rough clothes or leaving home, but they will mean putting wealth and status aside to some extent and embarking on a quest of our own to find the nature and cause of the world's problems.

What is the Problem?

A search for the causes of the global environmental crisis will take us through the realms of ecology, biology, climatology, politics, economics, sociology, and many other areas of knowledge. One could no doubt spend a lifetime reading up on the subject before getting around to doing anything to help. Let's begin by taking an objective overview of what the main environmental problems are:

Climate Change. The vast majority of scientific experts, while recognizing that uncertainties exist, believe that human-induced climate change is already occurring and that further change is inevitable. It is not a question of whether the earth's climate will change, but rather by how much, where, and how soon. Large parts of southern Africa, the Middle East, southern Europe, and Australia are likely to become more arid. In tropical and subtropical countries, agricultural production will decrease and diseases such as malaria and dengue will increase. Tens of millions of people (perhaps many more) will be displaced by rising sea levels. Delicate ecological systems such as coral reefs and forests will be endangered. Many believe the effects are already with us – that the increasing frequency of floods, droughts, and extreme weather events in recent years are human-induced.[4] Some scenarios are more serious still – the collapse of the Western Antarctic Ice Sheet into the sea could, for example, lead to a global sea level rise of ten metres, which would inundate major cities such as London.

Other Pollution. It is not just the headline-hitting incidents – such as oil spills and nuclear power plant disasters – that do the harm. Day by day, the poisoning of the air, land, rivers, and sea continues unpublicized. For example, each of us, on average, throws away ten times our own bodyweight in rubbish each year. If you add the amount of waste from manufacturing and delivery, the figure is nearer a hundred. Household rubbish is laced with toxic substances – chemicals, heavy metals from cleaning fluids, batteries, computers, PVC, and so on. Whether it is dumped in holes or burned, it lingers as a threat to human and animal health and has been blamed for increasing rates of cancer, birth defects, asthma, and allergies.

Species Extinction. It is undisputed that species are disappearing rapidly as their habitats are put under pressure from agriculture, pollution, urbanization, roads, and recreation. Biologists estimate the current rate of extinction to be between a hundred and a thousand times greater than it was before humans appeared. It also seems to be increasing. Elephants, tigers, pandas, mountain gorillas, and whales are already endangered, but the list includes many less enchanting varieties of plant, worm, beetle, and fungus, some of which are vital to medicine. The rapidly disappearing rosy periwinkle of Madagascar, for example, produces substances effective in treating leukaemia and Hodgkin's disease. While there have been isolated successes in rescuing species from extinction, in most cases conservation efforts have proved too little, too late.[5] The current mass extinction differs from those in the past because it is not only species that are being wiped out, but habitats. The pace of change is so fast that wildlife cannot migrate or adapt quickly enough to keep up.

Food and Water Shortages. As the world's population grows, pressure from food production increases. Numbers of fish and whales have been decimated by free-for-all industrial methods of exploitation. The great natural grasslands of Africa, North America, and Russia are being overgrazed. Mountain regions, such as the Himalayas and the Andes, are suffering from deforestation and soil erosion. Due to over-intensive farming methods, the fertile soil of some of the world's croplands is being blown away by the wind. Meanwhile, population is expected to grow by a quarter in the next twenty years, mostly in destitute, urban conditions, and the prospect of frequent famines grows more serious.[6] Even though we grow enough to feed everyone, there are 800,000,000 people in the world who are malnourished. There are also some 500,000,000 who don't have enough water, a figure that is expected to increase fivefold by 2025, as aquifers are pumped dry.

Searching for the causes

The debates about environmental causes and effects will no doubt run and run. But how much evidence does someone need before they decide that it's time to act? Whatever we conclude about the details, there is enough evidence to suggest that, at least as a matter of sensible precaution, radical changes are needed in our relationship to the environment. We need to look not just at the symptoms but also at the underlying causes.

One way of looking at the problem is in terms of our relationship to technology. The environmental problems we face have been brought about by the systematic overuse of increasingly powerful technologies. The internal combustion engine and agricultural mechanization came about to help people travel more easily and to grow more food. But what may be beneficial to the individual, when replicated by millions begins to have harmful consequences for everyone. New inventions set up whole new patterns of resource use and pollution, and enable social and political changes that are practically impossible to reverse. People have not necessarily set out to do harm, but they have not been able to foresee – or have chosen to ignore – the effects of their actions, preferring to leave it to someone else to sort out. In recent decades these effects have begun to take on global proportions. Like the Sorcerer's Apprentice, we have unleashed a magic we cannot control. We have unwittingly invented the means to wreak large-scale and irreversible havoc upon our home planet.

Technology will itself change. Even if we were to solve the problems associated with cars or agricultural chemicals, it is likely that new technologies with large-scale environmental effects would come along to take their place. The environmental crisis is to do with how we use technology, how and why we develop technology, and who benefits. Perhaps, as it's not the environment that's at fault, we could better describe the environmental crisis as a technological crisis.

However, we can't just blame technology. What about the people who invent, operate, or own the technology? Some environmentalists have condemned the human race in general, likening it to a virus on the face of the planet. Some schools of environmentalist thought have highlighted one simple cause, putting the blame on one group or another by virtue of their class, gender, or nationality.

But is the question of blame even the right one to be asking? The point, as Karl Marx observed, is not to interpret the world, but to change it.[7] Or, as Siddhartha might have put it, the quest is not to analyse suffering, but to end it. For me, the question is not so much whether any of the different theories of environmentalism are right or wrong, but whether they offer a prospect for change that can actually be realized. In this respect, they all lead, in one way or another, to one challenge – that of human motivation. However change occurs, it will do so because people learn to behave differently. Whatever our analysis of the environmental crisis, and whatever historic causes we choose to emphasize, this challenge cannot be ignored. In the end, it's not an environmental or a technological crisis we're facing – it's a human crisis.

How do you motivate people to change? Or more to the point, how do you even motivate yourself to change? Why should you bother? Why should you take responsibility for other people or for the natural world? How will this make you happier?

Let's return to the figure of Siddhartha leaving the palace. He did so, as we have seen, because he felt hemmed in. The discomfort of leaving the palace and going to live in the wilderness was as nothing compared to the frustration he would have felt if he had stayed. For him, it seems, the desire to help others was as natural as the desire of a lion to roam free. Was Siddhartha fundamentally different to the rest of us in this respect? He himself would say not – he was not a god or a prophet, just an ordinary human being. Is there anything in our own experience that resonates with his sense of being restricted?

You can only answer that question for yourself. I suspect it's a question that takes some thinking about, as we very easily get so used to limitation that we cease to be fully aware of it. I can see it in my own experience in a number of ways, especially in relation to the kind of lifestyle that is portrayed as the norm or the ideal by the media and advertising industry. Because Westernized societies are characterized by high-consumption lifestyles, they give rise to a collective sense of limitation. The flip side of materialism is boredom, anxiety, and guilt.

Boredom arises when we believe the message we are given that possessions – houses, cars, computers – will ultimately make us happy. This can lead us to invest too much of our hopes of happiness in the wrong things. In Britain, people make fun of train-spotters, but is this so different from getting hung up about different models of car or other kinds of gadgetry? Sooner or later, we grow bored and want the upgraded model. These are no more likely to give us lasting satisfaction than the number on the side of a railway engine.

In the wake of boredom comes anxiety. We have to spend time, money, and mental energy keeping up the payments on our possessions: protecting them, insuring them, and so on. In the background lies the knowledge that the whole economic system that supports Western lifestyles has to be protected by huge military forces. I clearly remember my primary school teacher telling us for the first time about nuclear weapons. It marked the arrival of a dull sense of anxiety that, notwithstanding the end of the Cold War, has never gone away. I suspect we are all so used to anxiety that we have come to think of it as normal.

Guilt arises because, despite our sophisticated attempts to ignore it, we know instinctively that there is some connection between our high-consumption lifestyles and poverty and environmental degradation. We know that we could do more to alleviate poverty. We know the rubbish we carelessly throw away has to go somewhere. We know that exhaust fumes pollute the air. In ordinary, everyday actions, we are adding to the residue of guilt. We are alienating ourselves from humanity and the natural world.

Boredom, anxiety, and guilt – these three poisons of materialist societies – imprison us to an extent we're probably not aware of. To the extent that we have succeeded in relegating them to the edge of our consciousness we have become comfortably numb. They prevent us from having a happy and straightforward relationship with other people and with the world around us.

So to continue our search for causes, what are the causes of boredom, anxiety, and guilt? How did we come to imprison ourselves so? How do we become free?

Waking Up

Siddhartha Gautama, living in a forest 2,500 years ago, asked himself exactly such questions. Having sought out the most renowned spiritual teachers of his time, he learned how to meditate and how to try to break through to the meaning of life through extreme physical hardships and fasting. He gained a reputation as an ascetic himself. In time, though, he saw that such extremes of austerity weren't helping him at all and that he was no nearer to finding the answers to his questions.

Sensing that a middle way would be a more fruitful approach, he started eating moderately again and embarked on a period of deep meditation. It was in the course of this that, sitting beneath a tree, he found that he was able to let go of the very last vestiges of greed, hatred, and unawareness. He had let go, once and for all, of seeing reality from a self-centred point of view. Hardly daring to believe that he had reached the end of his quest, he reached out his right hand and gently touched the earth with the tips of his fingers. As if the earth itself confirmed the reality of what had happened, his last remaining doubt evaporated. He experienced perfect clarity of mind, which was naturally accompanied by unbounded compassion for all living things. This was the awakening of his heart and mind to a state of utter peace and freedom from suffering. From then on, he became known as the Buddha, the 'Awakened One'.

According to the most accurate description he could give within the constraints of language, the key to the Buddha's liberation was the profound significance and reality of change. This was expressed in that part of his teaching often referred to as conditioned co-production: that everything that goes on in the universe is a constant flow of interdependent networks of causes and effects. Every single thing, on every level, from the smallest to the grandest scale, from second to second and aeon to aeon, comes about on the basis of a set of conditions; take away the conditions, and it ceases to exist. As a result, nothing is immune from change and, ultimately, everything affects everything else.

Why is this so radical and important? From our limited points of view, we want to believe that we are always going to be here in our present form and that things are always going to be the way we want them. Reality constantly reminds us that this is not the case. The world changes faster than we are comfortable with. We ourselves change from one day to the next, from one second to the next – our moods, our thoughts, our bodies. For all of us there exists the ever-present prospect of disease, old age, and death. But we do our best to ignore it. We might see intellectually that everything is subject to change, but we don't accept it emotionally.

We try to grasp things that we think will give us a permanent satisfaction. And if something or somebody gets in the way, we can react with aversion. Thus our stubborn unawareness of change is bound up with greed, hatred, fear, and anxiety. These are, in turn, bound up with suffering because, at heart, they represent a tension between reality and us.

The environmental crisis arises from the same tension. We want to believe that the natural world is so expansive that we can treat it as we wish without fear of the consequences. We want to believe that problems will be sorted out without any effort or sacrifice on our part. We want to carry on buying things without thinking about the effects on other people. We want to believe that there are unlimited sources of energy, clean water, and food. We want to believe that the sky is big enough to take all our pollution. For all its social, economic, and scientific complexity, what the environmental crisis boils down to is greed, hatred, and unawareness. These are the roots of boredom, anxiety, and guilt.

To let go of these fantasies would require us to make difficult decisions that we'd rather not face up to, so the fantasies are self-perpetuating. Greed, hatred, and unawareness are habits by which we limit our own happiness and freedom. Like any habit, they take time to let go of, but over time we can learn to let go of the idea that the me 'in here' is ultimately separate and different from other people and the universe 'out there'. We can experience ourselves as part of nature. We can become more compassionate, and, as there is no fixed law saying that particular beings have to experience a given amount of misery, we are free to become happier. In fact, there is no limit to how happy we are allowed to become – all we need is the means to do so. The world does not have to be in the state it is. Change is possible.

Imagine a world freed from poverty, war, and pollution. Never mind, for a moment, whether or not this is impossible idealism. Imagine the sense of joy and relief – it would be like a thousand Berlin Walls collapsing.

If that's too difficult, imagine yourself on your deathbed, looking back on your life. Imagine you've made some effort to change things, to live in greater harmony with others and with nature. The world's problems may not be solved, but you know in your heart that you've done what you could to make the world a better place. Compare that to how you'd feel if you knew you'd gone on being part of the problem, blindly hoping that someone else would sort out the mess.

Individually, we need to wake up from our habits of greed, hatred, and unawareness. Collectively, we need to wake up from our boredom, anxiety, and guilt. But is such change really possible? How could it come about? Even if I could change myself, surely that would not be enough – how do I change the world as well?

Changing Ourselves

The Buddha saw the vast potential range of the human condition. The same species that can degrade its home planet can also devote itself to saving it. The same goes for individuals. We often blind ourselves to this. We often demonize some people and sanctify others, as if we want to put them in a separate category from ourselves. We think of people as saints or messiahs, or monsters possessed by some special evil. The Buddha had a less fixed view of what and who we are. He taught that, in each second, with everything that we do, think, and say, we are shaping ourselves. We become what we do. With every act of greed, hatred, or unawareness, we develop qualities of selfishness and narrow-mindedness. With every act of love and kindness, we develop qualities of empathy and clarity. If we do any of these consistently enough, we can become greedy destroyers or bringers of peace. There are no limits, and everyone is free to change.

In Buddhism, the human state is regarded as immensely precious, precisely because it offers the potential for further development. The Buddha taught that this potential is limitless, that wisdom and compassion have no bounds. However much we already have these qualities, there are always new horizons. Each new day is an opportunity to explore our potential further. Complacency and moral superiority only distract us from the journey.

The Buddha set out a very practical path by which we can progressively liberate ourselves from our self-limiting habits. It includes meditation, together with a way of training ourselves to behave towards the world with non-violence and more loving-kindness. I'll say more about this later.

Changing the World

Looked at in the broader sweep of history, humankind has reached a crossroads. The long process of biological and mental evolution has endowed us with the capacity for a high degree of self-awareness. At some point, natural selection conferred a survival advantage on those primates with a greater capacity for introspection, probably because it helped to predict the behaviour of others. Since then, we have been able to imagine what it might be like to be someone else and how they might view us.[8] We have become the universe aware of itself.

Whether we use this capacity for self-awareness and empathy is up to us. Your own experience of it may be sporadic – some days you feel clearer and kinder than on other days. It has also waxed and waned through history – some cultures have prized and developed it, whereas others have neglected it. Those that have valued it tend towards civilization and co-operation, while those that have neglected it tend towards exploitation and control. The choice we face now may be very stark indeed – between a leap forward in the cultivation of awareness on the one hand and self-inflicted extinction on the other.

Some people think that Buddhism is just a path to individual peace of mind, a selfish escape from the realities of the world. This could hardly be further from the truth; the Buddha taught that real happiness comes from waking up to how we are connected with others. His teachings help us to find greater happiness not only for ourselves, but also for others – the two go together. They give us the means not only to change ourselves, but also to change the world.

Realizing that he had found the path to end the suffering of human existence, the Buddha devoted the rest of his life to helping others to follow in his footsteps. Cutting across the boundaries of caste and gender, he walked from place to place in northern India, teaching and befriending beggars, kings, warriors, courtesans, murderers, and priests. There are many stories about these encounters; the picture that emerges is one of a man without any of the affectations of a pseudo-spiritual teacher, without glibness or pride. He did not consider himself above helping a sick disciple. He had an intuitive understanding of people which enabled him to communicate with them in whatever way was appropriate – gentle words, blunt directness, rational argument, or a kindly, ironic humour. By the time he passed away, aged about eighty, he had followers from all sections of society across northern India, and he had started a spiritual tradition that was to spread down the centuries and across the world.

The Buddha not only inspired individual men and women, but, as a natural consequence, the society in which he lived. His world was dominated by the caste system, which condemned many people to demeaning servitude from birth until death. The Buddha refused to have anything to do with caste, and urged his followers to do likewise.[9] The effect of this was that, as his teachings spread, many people liberated themselves from caste. Even in modern-day India, a revival of the Buddha's teachings has given new hope and self-respect to millions of people formerly regarded as being of the lowest, so-called 'Untouchable', Hindu caste. The Buddha exerted this influence on history not by trying to take control of society, but by uncompromisingly exemplifying a more positive ideal.

The Buddha's teachings offer a practical means to unlock our own potential for changing the world. This is why they have so much to offer the environmental movement at this point in its history. Environmentalists have achieved successes in the last forty years or so on a heroic scale. They have established worldwide campaigning organizations, they have brought issues to the public's attention, they have educated people in how to begin to make things better by changing their own lives, or by being 'green consumers'. They have brought ideas such as sustainable development (development that meets present-day needs without compromising the ability of future generations to meet theirs) into schools, boardrooms, and the corridors of power.

But many environmentalists now feel they are coming up against the brick walls of political inertia and entrenched economic interest. The failure to reach complete international agreement on the reduction of carbon emissions has been a case in point. Government decisions have been taken in the short-term profit-making interests of large corporations rather than in the interest of the common good. Increasingly, the big environmental issues are bound up with the global disparities of wealth and power. The writer Tom Athanasiou has remarked that the fundamental political truth of our time is that the change that is necessary is not realistic – that is to say, it is not regarded as realistic.[10] While many people understand the need for change, bringing it about is another matter. The environmental movement is becoming aware of this as its new priority. It is not enough to alert the public to the facts; somehow we need to motivate them to act. As a former director of Greenpeace puts it, 'We know that the world is burning. The question is how to put out the fire.'"

Awakening Hearts and Minds: The Bodhisattva Path

What we need is a way of not only waking ourselves from our self-limiting habits, but also waking the rest of the world from fixed ways of thinking. It needs to be a practical path rather than a distant ideology. It needs to end in what seem to be impossible dreams of world harmony and a clean planet, but it needs to begin where we are now, with all our doubts and imperfections.

The process of awakening the heart and mind is such a path. One of the names accorded to it by the Buddhist tradition is the path of the Bodhisattva. A Bodhisattva is 'one who strives for awakening' not merely for his or her own sake but for the sake of all living beings. As an ideal, the Bodhisattva is often portrayed as the epitome of altruism, utterly dedicated to the welfare of the world.

Ideals can sometimes seem a very long way off, but anyone can begin to be a Bodhisattva. The Bodhisattva path – the path of learning and awakening – can start anywhere. It promises greater happiness on the most humble as well as the most elevated level, and it requires no blind faith in some distant ideal. It consists in the steady cultivation of the qualities of generosity, ethical conduct, forbearance, energy, meditation, and wisdom.[12] I will say more about these in the next few chapters.

As well as being a way to greater personal happiness, the Bodhisattva path offers a way to equip ourselves for the task of effectively addressing the environmental crisis. It is a way of training ourselves in the qualities we will need if we are really going to make a difference.

three

ONLY CONNECT!

There are many practical ways of living more in harmony with nature, and I'll be looking at some of these in the next chapter. But living in harmony with nature is inseparable from living in harmony with each other. It's not just a question of somehow bolting environmental awareness on to our existing lifestyles. Environmental problems, with their roots in greed, hatred, and unawareness, should cause us to question our whole way of being in the world. When the Buddha saw that we are not ultimately separate from the universe or from others, it was not just an intellectual observation. His realization that all things are interconnected was something felt in his heart as much as his head, and it moved him to live out the rest of his life helping others.[13]

If we experience a desire to do something to help the environment, it is probably because we ourselves have to some extent understood interconnectedness. According to the Buddha, this is something we can grow to understand more and more deeply. We can do this by trying it out, little by little, through individual acts of kindness. If we are truly interconnected, these will make us on the whole freer and happier. In this chapter, I'd like to examine how this sense of exploration might bring to life our whole approach to the environment.

The Armchair Society

In the West, people have become ever more oriented to material consumption, and live in smaller and smaller units. The average number of people in each household is steadily declining. If the trends continue much further, we will soon all be sitting in our own armchair, in our own house, watching our own television. The information age, progressing through the successive technologies of radio, television, the Internet, and mobile phones, is reaching the point of saturation, where everyone has instant access to virtually unlimited information. We have televisions in the kitchen and the bedroom, computers on our palms, and telephones in our pockets. In turn, each new technology has become the object of fetishistic desire, as status symbol or fashion statement. All too often, the actual content of the information having been transmitted, the quality of our communication becomes of secondary or no importance at all. Indeed, the very quantity of information at our fingertips can numb our minds to the whole notion of quality. The television addict, the computer nerd, and the loud but vacuous mobile phone user have become the successive icons of the passing decades.

It is not just information that we expect to have at our command. We expect fast food, fast transport, fast service. We expect a wide array of choices of even the most everyday products. I heard a story of an East European woman who was visiting England. Faced with the bewildering array of different kinds of shampoo on a supermarket shelf, she burst into tears. Yet choice is what we've come to expect and consider normal. We would probably like to think of ourselves as an exception – it's other people who are the rampant materialists, who are obsessed with information and gadgets. But I wonder whether it might apply to all of us more than we'd like to acknowledge. When you are brought up within a particular culture, you unconsciously imbibe its values and habits. We can come to consider the strangest things quite normal.

The writer Helena Norberg-Hodge lived for many years in the Himalayan kingdom of Ladakh. It is a place that had, until the advent of the Westernized economy, a very strong sense of community and co-operation. Despite living in a land with few resources and a harsh climate, Ladakhis have a reputation for irrepressible happiness and laughter. Norberg-Hodge relates how, when told that many people in the affluent West were so unhappy they had to go to see their doctor, the Ladakhis' mouths dropped open in astonishment.[14]

How have we so spectacularly failed to build a happy society despite our material wealth? How can we begin to move forward? What are the unconscious assumptions that are holding us back?

We carry a model in our heads about the way we function in society, one that most of us rarely question. We see ourselves as tightly defined units, either individually or in households. To put it crudely, money comes into the unit at one end when we receive our wages and it goes out of the other when we buy things. Compared to other societies, our actual experience of being connected with others is slight. The advertising industry, which equates consumption with status, and the job market both promote an essentially competitive relationship between units. Somewhere along the line we have lost the art of living together.

In the post-industrial era, many of the cohesive forces in society have been weakened. There is much more geographical and social mobility – there are few who live and work with the same people, and families and friends tend to live further apart. Traditional rural communities and industrial working-class neighbourhoods have largely dispersed. There are few communities left where a unifying ideology, such as Christianity, socialism, or nationalism, can be taken for granted. The ideal of democracy, in so far as it is shared, allows us to live together but does not provide a common purpose, something higher than our private economic interests.

Our problem is that we are living as though disconnected. We think we are disconnected from our neighbours, from people in other countries, from the natural world. But this isn't in accord with reality – it doesn't work. Everything we eat and drink comes from the earth. We depend on others in countless ways even for the most basic necessities of life. But, too often, we just want to look after our own little unit. And the more we have withdrawn into our own private sphere, the more boredom, loneliness, or desire for status has driven us to consume.

We now have a choice. One option is to sit in our armchair and accept the ascendancy of untrammelled capitalism, with all its social and environmental problems. Another is to try to escape to an imagined utopia away from it all, a rustic idyll where we can turn back the clock. A third option is to begin to build within our society a new cohesion, co-operation, and trust from first principles, based not on an imposed ideology but on our common humanity. This means patiently beginning the work of rebuilding. It means connecting with people, as a way of trying out the truth of interconnectedness.

To begin this patient work of rebuilding, we can reflect on how we affect other people individually and on how we affect the world as a whole. Having done so, we can make a conscious effort to connect with people in a more positive way by giving.

How do I Affect Other People?

Every time you speak to someone, buy something from them, or just sit opposite them on a train, you are sending out ripples of cause and effect into the world. The effects are sometimes positive, sometimes negative. Being preoccupied with our own concerns, we all too often forget this, but as part of the process of learning and awakening, we can train ourselves to think more about it. I'll come back to this later. The point I want to make here is that it's not just our deliberately willed actions that affect others. We are constantly communicating with others across a much broader spectrum than simply our words – through every minor detail of our body and speech. We communicate who we are as well as what we do; we communicate our lifestyle, our state of mind, our values. The Vietnamese monk Thich Nhat Hanh illustrates this with an image of some refugee 'boat people' adrift on the ocean:

> Often the boats are caught in rough seas or storms, the people may panic, and boats can sink. But if even one person aboard can remain calm, lucid, knowing what to do and what not to do, he or she can help the boat survive. His or her expression – face, voice – communicates clarity and calmness, and people have trust in that person. They will listen to what he or she says. One such person can save the lives of many.[15]

When we talk with other people about environmental issues or the state of the world, it is not just what we are saying that makes a difference, but how we are saying it. We can communicate panic and despair, or clarity and calm. The communication of panic and despair follows from a desire to take from other people a sense of reassurance or comfort. The communication of clarity and calm follows from a desire to work with others to find a solution. These are two very different kinds of environmentalism.

We can see this even in very ordinary circumstances. If you have ever worked with someone in a very negative state of mind, you will know how this casts a cloud over everyone. Conversely, just the occasional friendly word on a train can dispel the atmosphere of reserve and make for a more relaxed and enjoyable journey for everyone.

A Reflection

Take some time to reflect on what you communicate to others, how you connect to others across this broad spectrum through your body language and tone of voice. You may be fortunate and know someone whom you could ask and who will give you an honest answer.

Consider in particular whether you transmit calm or anxiety, clarity or confusion, friendliness, reserve, or ill will. Communicate a natural concern when talking about environmental issues, rather than despair. Think back to people who have had a positive influence on your life. What was it about their communication that affected you? Could you affect others in a similar way?

How Do I Change the World?

As well as thinking we are disconnected from others, we very often think we are disconnected from the world at large. To use the words of the political thinker André Gorz, we feel 'impotent in the face of autonomized processes and faceless powers'.[16] We tend to think that the world is only really changed by people in positions of wealth and power. This is certainly the view perpetrated by the news media, which can often whip up the most trivial murmur in circles of government as if it were a matter of great national import.

But this is a very narrow way of thinking about how change occurs, and one that makes us feel so marginal and unimportant that we can be misled into thinking that our own actions don't have consequences. An alternative view is that acts of parliament or international treaties come about because of the forces of public opinion – or perhaps something deeper than just opinion. People's values and perceptions, individually and collectively, can shift in quite mysterious and unpredictable ways. The sum total of the broad spectrum of communications going on, by which people communicate their values and states of mind, will have an effect. In this light, formal politics can look more like what the writer Tor Nørretranders has described as 'tardy rationalizations of what has already taken place'.[17] He cites as an example the end of the mutual paranoia that underpinned the Cold War. In the mid-1980s, he argues, even before the break-up of the Soviet bloc, there was a defusing of tension that could not be explained by any formal political process. He speculates that this was the result of millions of ordinary people, persistently, over the decades, talking about the unthinkable nature of nuclear war. In unseen ways, they brought about a phase transition that changed history. In this perspective, politicians just bumble along a few years behind the cutting edge of change. Human society is as complex and chaotic as any ecosystem. We may think that our behaviour, conversations, and transactions are our own private business, but, in aggregate, they are constantly bringing about changes in ways we don't even suspect. You don't have to win an election or stage a revolution to change the world. Our actions do have consequences.

This isn't to say that political activity, such as environmental campaigning, isn't necessary, but we shouldn't lose sight of how we affect people in very ordinary ways. Having high ideals about saving the environment is not necessarily enough; one could spend one's whole life talking and thinking about ideas, bold plans, utopian visions, but without a way of putting them into practice – at least to some extent – they have been not the slightest bit of use to anybody. There is a danger with big issues such as the global environment that you lose yourself in abstractions. You might even entertain private fantasies about saving the world single-handedly. You can convince yourself that you have great concern for the world, when actually you can't even get along with the people you see every day.

A Sharing Revolution

What are the ordinary individual words and deeds that will bring about a phase transition towards an environmentally sustainable future? If lack of connection lies at the heart of the problem, it follows that the most direct antidotes are things that start to reconnect us, such as giving and sharing. The quality of generosity is rarely mentioned in environmentalist writings, yet it has never been so indispensable. Giving material things reminds us that happiness comes from connecting with others. Sharing things breaks down the barriers of our isolated consumer units.

Giving and sharing are powerful acts because they undermine the notion, taken for granted by some economists, that we all act out of economic self-interest and that economic growth is the greatest good. On a world scale, these qualities will be expressed as a global vision of fairness and security, which will counter the attitude, still advanced by leading politicians, that the national economic interest should always take precedence over global concerns. Economists can only measure financial transactions and too easily forget that happiness does not equate with how much money we spend.[18]

Generosity is a kind of liberation movement. Liberation movements arise when people refuse to assent any longer to whatever regime or ideology is oppressing them. The idea of freedom becomes contagious and pressure for change becomes irresistible. If materialism and isolation are the great oppressions of Western society, then generosity is liberation.

So the first step forward can be taken through the very ordinary and simple act of generosity. Anyone can do it. Even someone in the most self-absorbed state, if they put their mind to it, can find some way of giving, even if it's just a tiny gesture of friendliness. This is the first step towards rejoining the human race, connecting with others. It relieves us from the narrow, constricted pain of selfish isolation.

Progressively, starting from wherever we are and working upwards, we can try out more ways of freeing ourselves. At each stage, we can reflect on how generosity feels, not in a self-righteous way, but feeling what it's like to be more connected to other human beings. If you have ever worked in a situation where everyone is pulling together, or played in a band, or been part of a sports team, you may recall sometimes thinking in terms of 'us' rather than 'me'. We can look to develop this sense of 'us-ness' in our everyday lives, beginning with those around us, then including more and more people. Here are some examples of giving and sharing, many of which have an environmental flavour:

- Give a gift to your neighbour.

- Pick up a piece of litter every day.

- Share garden tools.

- Start a car-sharing scheme.

- Adopt a development charity to give to, or volunteer for.

- Offer your services via a local or international volunteer bureau.[19]

- Adopt a local green space and help to improve it.

- Become a conservation volunteer.[20]

- Join a LETS (local exchange trading scheme) or a skills co-operative.[21]

There are many other things we could do, of course. Perhaps as we go on, we'll find that we want to increase the amount of time and energy we give to them. This is one way of responding to the environmental crisis – learning to connect with others more and more. A sharing society will tend to live in greater harmony with nature.

In the Buddhist scriptures there is a story about three disciples of the Buddha who were living in a wooded place called Gosinga.[22] One day, the Buddha came to visit. He first enquired after their physical well-being and then asked whether they were living together in harmony. He was pleased to find that they were bearing each other in mind so naturally that no words about practical tasks were needed. The first to return from the almsround would fetch drinking water, and the last would wash the refuse bucket. Whoever noticed that the washing water was low would fetch more. Each would maintain the attitude that while they were different in body they were one in mind. Being sensitive to nature, they took care that no waste was discarded wherever there was greenery or water that supported life. For the three disciples, devoted to simplicity and meditation, complete harmony with each other and with their environment was the foundation of a truly human existence.

four

SIMPLIFY, SIMPLIFY

Having given some thought to how we might get into the habit of being more connected to others, the next question is – what specific things do we need to do? How should one's lifestyle be changed to help the environment? Most books of this kind will include a list of environmental dos and don'ts. This one is no exception, so here it is – a list of twenty-five specific things you can do that will make a difference. A lot of them are one-off actions that will have lasting consequences. You could set yourself a timescale, say a month, and put a reminder in your diary to check how many you've done. But please read the rest of the chapter before you start, because I'll be suggesting that it's not just what you do, but how and why you do it, that makes a difference.[23]

Twenty-Five Excellent Things To Do

See how many of these action points you can tick off after a month. Most of them can be carried out in any country, though most of the information references and phone numbers are UK-based.

- Make a decision to avoid air travel whenever possible. Calculate the carbon emissions from your flight at **www. chooseclimate.org/flying/index.html**

- If you drive, set a target to cut down on car mileage – a 25% reduction could save a tonne of greenhouse gases in a year.

- Drive at 50 mph instead of 70 mph and save 25% on fuel.

- Try out public transport alternatives for your most frequent journeys and find ways to enjoy the ride.

- Take up cycling, especially for local journeys. To join a peaceful bike-power protest, visit **www. critical-mass.org**

- Phosphate-filled detergents kill plant and fish life – use alternatives such as eco-balls (from **www. ecozone.co.uk**), which contain no harmful chemicals at all.

- Clean your house without polluting the environment. Look out for environmentally friendly labelling or check out the available products at **www.greenpeace.org.uk/products/toxics** or **www.arcania.co.uk/greentree/features/clean.htm**

- Wash your clothes at 40°C maximum – any hotter is unnecessary.

- Turn down your central heating thermostat by 1°C.

- Check your insulation and find out some other energy saving ideas through the Energy Savings Trust (**www.saveenergy. co.uk** 0845 727 7200). You could save up to £200 a year on your bills.

- Switch to green electricity. It is now possible to use electricity from only renewable sources – try Unit-e (**www. unit-e.co.uk** 0845 601 1410) or check out more options through Friends of the Earth (**www.foe.co.uk/campaigns/ climate/issues/green_energy** 020 7490 1555).

- Check out green DIY and building products through the Association for Environment Conscious Building (**www. aecb.net** 01559 370908) or the Green

Building Store (**www.greenbuilding store.co.uk** 01484 854898).

- Become an ethical consumer – make a start by informing yourself of the options. For general information contact Ethical Consumer (**www. ethical consumer.org** 0161 226 2929), or Ethical Junction (**www.ethical-junction.org** 0161 236 3637), or Get Ethical (**www. getethical.com**).

- Specific sources include the Organic Consumers' Association (**www. organicconsumers.org** USA +1 218 226 4164), the Clean Clothes Campaign (**www.cleanclothes.org** Netherlands +31 20 4122 785), the Fairtrade Foundation (**www.fairtrade. org** 020 7405 5942), the National Recycling Forum (**www.nrf.org.uk/buy-recycled/nrf/ credit.htm**), the Green Stationery Company (**www.greenstat. co.uk** 01225 480556). Afterwards, reward yourself with a special treat of some **www. divinechocolate.com**

- Prepackaged sandwiches and bottled drinks are wasteful of materials and energy, as well as expensive. Get into the habit of making your own and buy your own water bottle.

- Take your own shopping bag and refuse excess packaging.

- Start a compost heap, preferably built from scrap materials. Remember that they benefit from fibre such as tissues and cereal boxes as well as uncooked food. Contact Waste Watch for tips (**www.wastewatch.org.uk** 0870 243 0136).

- Choose slow food rather than fast food – take time to enjoy growing, preparing, and eating food. To really make a meal of it, check out **www.slowfood.com**

- Put arrangements in place for a green burial. For full information on pollution-free funerals and biodegradable coffins, contact the Natural Death Centre (**www.naturaldeath.co.uk** 020 8208 2853).

- Make yours a pesticide-free wildlife garden. Contact the Henry Doubleday Research Association for information (**www.hdra.org.uk** 02476 303517). Many species of butterflies are endangered – find out how to help them through Butterfly Conservation (**www.butterfly-conservation.org.uk** 01929 400209).

- Grow your own flowers or give plants instead of commercially produced flowers. They are often associated with heavy pesticide use, cheap labour, and high transport-related pollution.

- Ask your bank whether it has an ethical investment policy. If not, switch to the Co-op (**www.co-operativebank.co.uk** 0161 832 3456) or Triodos (**www.triodos. co.uk** 0117 973 9339) and tell your old bank why you changed. For other ethical investment advice, see **www. ethicalmoney.org**

- Eliminate junk mail. If you register with the Mailing Preference Service (Freepost 22, London W1E 7EZ, 020 7766 4410), they will remove your name from mailing lists.

- Contact your MP or local councillor on an environmental issue, such as road building or local recycling facilities.

- Support a development charity or campaign. Here are a few examples to choose from: WaterAid (**www.wateraid. org.uk** 020 7793 4500), the World Development Movement (**www.wdm. org.uk** 020 7737 6215), Oxfam (**www. oxfam.org.uk** 01865 312610), or for a Buddhist-run alternative dedicated to dignity and self-confidence, the Karuna Trust (**www.karuna.org** 020 7700 3434).

- Find out lots more excellent things to do: send away for the book from which many of the above ideas were drawn: *Go Mad: 365 Daily Ways to Save the Planet*, published by *The Ecologist* (**www. theecologist.org** 01795 414963).

Lists such as these are an excellent place to start and give us plenty of good, practical things to be getting on with, but there are some drawbacks to just ticking off boxes. First, lists in themselves don't motivate us to take action. Even if we do take action, we don't always sustain it. Most of us who have made New Year's resolutions know how easy it is to slip back into our unwanted habits by February.

Secondly, it is all too easy to select the least challenging things on the list and ignore the rest. For example, it is tempting to think that by recycling one's glass and paper, one is 'doing one's bit for the environment'. Whilst recycling reduces the amount of waste that is incinerated or dumped in local landfill sites, it has little or no impact on big global issues such as climate change. If you're making a special car journey to the recycling bank, it might even have a negative effect. It is easy to espouse an environmental sentimentality whilst quietly putting off decisions that are really going to bite. We need to be clear about what we're doing and why. There needs to be a clear relationship between the precise problems we want to address and the actions we take. The well-known slogan 'Think Global, Act Local' only works if the action taken locally is appropriate to the global problems.

A third pitfall of lists of dos and don'ts is that they can reduce environmental concern to a matter of following rules. The problem of following rules is that you can forget the original motivation for doing so and it becomes a very dry experience. There's a danger of becoming a bit of an eco-bore. You've probably met the kind of person who sternly tells you off for putting your orange peel in the wrong compost bin. Or worse, you might have found yourself doing it to others. This type of 'environmental correctness' probably does more harm than good. How many of us are so perfect that we are in a position to judge others? In any case, what is an easy decision for us might require a real effort for someone else. A morally superior attitude singularly fails to inspire other people to take action. Perhaps the best thing to do if you find it creeping into your own thinking is to throw your jam jars into the main rubbish bin for a day or two, and enjoy the sense of freedom! To avoid these pitfalls, we need to keep the following points in mind when we try to apply an action list:

- Don't let the fact that you can't be perfect stop you from doing anything at all. We can all make a start somewhere.

- Remain aware of your basic motivation. What motivates you positively? Is it, for example, a concern for wildlife, or a desire that people should be able to live happily on the earth in the future?

- Do the unexpected. If you find yourself dismissing certain actions as too difficult, gently ask yourself why. It is likely to be the difficult things (usually those that have implications for the way we spend our time or money) that break the more harmful patterns of our lives and really make a difference. Work up to doing at least one thing that is quite radical and unexpected, despite the difficulties.

- Don't rest on your laurels. There is always something more to do.

- Don't get stuck in guilt. Enjoy doing what you can and try to make progress. What a difference it would make if everyone did that.

- Cultivate simplicity. Don't think of the action list as an end in itself, but as a guideline for cultivating a richer, more contented lifestyle, in tune with the environment and with others.

In the rest of this chapter, I'll look at these areas in more depth and see how the Buddha's teachings might give us some insight into them.

Motivation:
The Cultivation of Wisdom and Compassion

What motivates us to take action on the environment in the first place? In some way, it is probably a desire to end suffering, particularly the suffering that comes from the pollution, stress, and exploitation associated with the environmental crisis. We see people struggling to survive drought, or animals losing their habitats, and something inside us is moved to respond. Something resonates.

This basic desire that other beings should not come to harm is what underlies Buddhist ethics. There are no commandments in Buddhism – just a set of guidelines to help us cultivate non-violent and loving states of mind. The things that lead us to such states, covering actions of body, speech, and mind, are:

- acts of kindness,

- open-handed generosity,

- stillness, simplicity, and contentment,

- truthful communication,

- clear and radiant awareness.

Underlying these is the principle of non-violence. The Buddha himself exemplified it. Not only did he oppose the iniquities of the caste system of his day, but he also repeatedly spoke against the practice of blood sacrifice.[24] There is some evidence that the Buddha's teachings brought about a change of attitude towards animals throughout India, even within his own lifetime, which endures today. Non-violence is difficult or even impossible to apply in an absolute way. Just being alive implicates us in the death of countless micro-organisms inside our bodies. There are many situations in the world – violent crime, state brutality, terrorism, war – in which it is hard to see a non-violent solution that does not itself imply more suffering. But these difficulties need not deter us from being as non-violent as we can, trying our best in each circumstance to see the best way forward. They don't undermine non-violence as a principle, but only go to demonstrate that we live in a world of complex choices, where we don't have the comfort of simplistic rules that will tell us what to do in every situation.

What we can do, over a period of time, is push back the boundaries of our sensitivity to other living things. In Buddhist ethics, what defines an act as positive or negative is not whether it conforms to a rule, but the motivation behind it. So non-violence is not a rule or an external observance, but a state of heart and mind. In each situation, we bring to bear whatever wisdom and compassion we have and try to act non-violently. From each situation, we learn how we might have done better, how we can become wiser and more compassionate. The Buddha likened this development of wisdom and compassion to lotuses growing from the mud. We may begin by being tightly closed and bound within mud, but we can start to reach out of the mud and up through the water. Eventually, we will rise above the surface of the pond and open up to the sunlight as beautifully coloured and fragrant flowers.

We can use our action list in the same way – not as a list of commandments to be obeyed out of grim duty, but as a tool to help us cultivate an attitude of non-violence to all that lives. To the extent that we can do this, our actions to help the environment will become a natural expression of our growing wisdom and compassion. They will become a celebration of life itself.

Doing the Unexpected

It is sometimes difficult enough to behave ethically even when face to face with those affected by one's actions. How much more difficult it is when separated by thousands of miles, or by decades or generations. This is exactly the predicament we face in the modern world. The complexities of manufacturing systems, technological processes, and trading patterns all obscure from us the effects of our actions. We don't know where our potatoes were grown, which forest our newspaper came from. We don't see the undesired effects of the chemicals we spray in our gardens. We may not even know what happens to our own effluent once it disappears round the U-bend.

It follows that to act truly ethically in the modern world will require some extra effort on our part. The changes we need to make to our lives are very real and visible, while the benefits they might have are far away and far removed. It is very easy in these circumstances to develop ethical blind spots – areas that we're dimly aware of but would rather not look into too closely. But if we do look at them, they can be seen as valuable opportunities, because these are exactly the changes that will have the most transformative effect on ourselves and the world.

We need to be willing to change our habits. People often fear that behaving in an environmentally friendly way means spending one's days lost in complex calculations of the effects of car exhausts, roof lagging, and plastic bags, continually weighing one course of action against another. But our lifestyles are really just an amalgam of habits. We don't usually decide from scratch on each new occasion which washing powder to buy or how to travel to work. With a little initial effort, habits can be changed. Perhaps we can have the greatest effect by keeping the environment in mind when making big decisions – where to live, how to make a living, where to go on holiday, and so on.

In this way, instead of necessarily thinking about changing everything at once, you could think about changing your habits and conditions over a period of time. You could, for example, make a list of proposed changes and make a note in your diary to review your progress every three months. The important thing is to remember why you want to make the changes, not to lose touch with your motivation. In this way, changing your lifestyle will be a natural part of broadening your sphere of concern. If this happens, making the right choices will become second nature.

A CASE STUDY: AIR TRAVEL

Let's take as an example the first point on our action list – air travel. Perhaps the most pressing global issue of the moment is climate change, the greenhouse effect. This is brought about by so-called greenhouse gases (mainly carbon dioxide) which we have been emitting in large quantities since the beginning of the Industrial Revolution and especially in the last fifty years. They reduce the amount of heat that the earth radiates back into space, leading to a gradual warming of the atmosphere. There are a number of ways in which you can reduce the levels of greenhouse gas emissions for which you are personally responsible. One of these is to avoid travelling by air, or at least to reduce your air mileage. Increasing numbers of people are travelling by air, which has led to a three per cent increase in greenhouse gas emissions per year.[25] You can cause as much greenhouse gas emission in one return transatlantic flight as in driving a car for a year. So, avoiding a rule-following approach, how can one engage one's imagination more with the consequences of air travel? There are two ways of doing this, both of which might help.

First, before booking a flight, visualize a square on the ground ten metres by ten, and imagine all the air above it, stretching up to the top of the atmosphere. The same amount of carbon dioxide is contained in that column of air as is emitted for each passenger on a 1,500-mile flight (roughly the distance from London to Athens). To absorb that amount of carbon dioxide, you would have to plant a tree that would grow to twelve metres in height.[26] Once emitted, the gas will stay in the atmosphere for more than a century, still, as it were, bearing your name on it.

Imagine meeting and talking with some of the people who, over that period, will lose their homes, their means of livelihood, or their lives, through rising sea levels, floods, and droughts brought about by global warming, and to which you have contributed. What would you say?

Imagine, again, being back in Tuvalu, talking with Tubwebwe (see chapter two). As she strains the nonu juice she talks about her anxiety as to what will become of her three children if their island is lost beneath the rising sea. She asks you why this might happen and whether you can help.

Imagine watching a nature documentary in a few decades' time describing the death of the last coral reef. How would you feel?

Imagine the effects that some scientists are warning of, in which some of the Antarctic ice sheet slips into the sea, leading to an even higher rise in sea levels than predicted for ordinary global warming scenarios, and deluging vast populated areas such as London. Or to take the worst scenario of all, imagine the fate of the last surviving people and animals struggling to find sustenance from an increasingly scorched planet.

Perhaps you have now decided not to buy the ticket, or you might have taken the consequences into account but decided they are outweighed by the benefits to the world of your journey (not something one could do lightly). You could still choose to travel overland by bus or train, or go by sea.

Perhaps you have dismissed the above scenarios as overly emotive, or even hysterical, even though they merely point out some very real possibilities. Or you could argue that the aircraft is travelling anyway and one extra passenger won't make any difference. Aircraft only fly, though, because passengers pay the airlines. Yours might be the booking (or cancellation) that makes the difference between a flight going ahead or not. We have individual responsibilities even in collective situations, a point which also accounts for the 'my little bit of greenhouse gas emissions won't make that much difference' argument.

Perhaps you feel concerned by the effects of air travel, but not concerned enough to make a difference to your decision. Thinking about the consequences only makes you feel guilty. To get this far is a very positive step if, instead of just feeling guilty, you recognize the limitations of your concern for others and resolve to do something about it.

Now try out the second way of imagining the consequences of all our actions. Imagine the earth in a few decades or centuries, home to happy, thriving human societies and a myriad colourful forms of life. Cultivate a care for the health of the planet, as you would care for the health of your own body. Think of yourself as the protector of coral reefs and future generations of people. Imagine talking to those future people and being able to say, 'I was one of those who helped to change things for the better.'

Using the Imagination: Some Other Examples

Similar exercises of the imagination can easily be devised with respect to other common choices we are faced with.

Car travel is another major contributor of greenhouse gases and other forms of pollution such as acid rain – a cocktail of photochemicals that has damaged vast stretches of forest and poisoned tens of thousands of lakes in Europe and North America. Pollution from cars also aggravates asthma and can cause eye irritation, coughs, and lung and chest problems. When you buy a new car, you are using up large quantities of finite resources in steel, plastic, aluminium, and rubber. Imagine the effects of all these on real people.

Keep in mind, if you do drive, that the houses, villages, and towns that pass like a blur outside the windows are people's homes, and how you drive affects their peace of mind and safety. Noise is a frequently overlooked aspect of environmental pollution. It is worth taking some time to think how one affects others in this respect, not only by the transport one uses, but also through stereos, barking dogs, security alarms, and so on.

The immediate effects of eating meat are quite easy to imagine, especially if you've ever visited a slaughterhouse. Many Buddhists are vegetarian simply because meat-eating involves the taking of life, but there are also very good environmental reasons for eating less meat. It is a grossly inefficient use of agricultural land – as much grain is fed to livestock in the United States as is consumed the populations of India and China put together.[27] Farm animals produce about a fifth of the methane (a greenhouse gas) in the atmosphere. About a hundred and fifty thousand square miles of the Amazon rainforest have been cleared for beef production.[28] This deforestation also contributes to global warming, because trees soak up carbon dioxide. Imagine the richness of the forests, or the people who could be fed as a result of using land more efficiently.

Experiments with Simplicity

If we practise environmentalism as a list of rules bolted on to our existing lifestyle, we might find it's an unwanted complication; just one more thing to think about. But if we use our imagination and think of it as a way of cultivating a richer connection with life, the opposite is likely to be true.

Many people in the West are locked into high-income high-consumption ways of life, working long hours to buy the best cars, holidays, and electronic gadgetry. Sometimes we get into self-perpetuating loops – earning the money to buy the car that we need for work; or to squeeze enough enjoyment out of one fortnight's holiday to compensate for overworking the rest of the year.

Some people have embraced the idea of 'voluntary simplicity' and made radical changes to their lifestyles, working less and consuming less. Some are motivated by environmental concerns, while others are escaping the rat race.

Many have found that their lives have been enriched – rather than impoverished – by the experience. It can reduce stress, sweep away a lot of the time-consuming clutter of life (buying, cleaning, maintaining, and insuring things), and encourage more creativity and communication.

The Buddha taught simplicity as a guideline for living because he knew how easily distracted we are, how easily we can get caught up in inconsequential detail. Being caught up in details alienates us from other people, or brings us into competition or conflict with them. The more we can open ourselves up to the question of how much is really necessary, the more likely we are to be in harmony with others and with the natural world.

Everyone can try some experiments with simplicity. Here are some examples of modest steps we could take towards lower consumption, most of which could be tried out for a week or two:

- Buy food in bulk and enjoy the art of cookery.

- Live without television, radio, and your computer.

- Ignore the news media for a while.

- Reduce working hours and use the extra free time creatively.

- Give up the idea of shopping as a leisure activity.

- Keep a note of what you spend your money on and see how much is really unnecessary.

- Get rid of things that are neither useful nor beautiful.

- Use public transport instead of a car, spending the time in reflection or reading.

Once you have tried these experiments, you might, if you have not already done so, feel more inclined to more radical courses of action, such as living without a car, changing your employment patterns, or living more communally.

The point is not to deny ourselves things, but to strip away some of the inessentials of life so that what is essential can shine through. Initially we might find ourselves bored without our usual distractions, or it may be that we have to ask ourselves what the essential is – what is life for if not to work and consume?

Practised in this way, simplicity is more than a way of avoiding stress or even of living in greater harmony with the environment. It is a way of streamlining our lives around their central purpose. As part of awakening the heart and mind, the process of simplification can be carried much further than choices of lifestyle. Ultimately, all our thoughts, words, and deeds can express non-harmfulness and loving-kindness – which become part of who we are as well as what we do. The Buddhist teacher Sangharakshita describes what he calls this aesthetic simplicity in the following way:

The truly simple life glows with significance, for its simplicity is not the dead simplicity of a skeleton but the living simplicity of a flower or a great work of art. The unessential has melted like mist from life and the Himalayan contours of the essential are seen towering with sublime simplicity above the petty hills and valleys of the futilities of mundane existence.[29]

five

THE TWO WINGS OF A BIRD

We have looked at some of the ways in which, through our day-to-day choices, we might make a difference to the environmental crisis. But is this enough? Will generosity and changes of lifestyle bring about change soon enough to prevent the disastrous consequences we fear? Should we not also be throwing ourselves into political campaigning and green activism? Are there other ways to help?

Some environmental problems are less likely to be affected just by lifestyle changes we make in the West. Species extinction is a prime example. The highest extinction rates occur through deforestation and over-intensive agriculture in developing countries, especially in South America. This are due in part to Western consumer demands for meat, hardwoods, and even exotic animals. Increasingly, though, this is brought about by pressure on agricultural land within those countries. Grain production is decreasing through soil erosion and urbanization, while populations are expanding rapidly. Experience has shown that the best way to stabilize population growth is through education and family planning. Agriculture can be helped through investment in appropriate technology. The scale of change necessary requires action by Western governments in the areas of development aid, Third World debt, and international trading relations.

Governmental action can have an effect beyond that of individuals, as in the case of the Montreal Protocol on the emission of ozone-depleting chemicals. So while we can't rely on governments to take prompt action or provide leadership on environmental issues, neither can we leave this entirely to individuals. We need to find ways to influence our governments, not to mention the banks and multinational corporations, to take action.

There are many ways to take the initiative with environmental issues, some political, and some not:

- Become involved in conservation work, or plant some trees.

- Become involved in environmental education.

- Get a job that actively promotes environmental awareness.

- Support or become active in a Third World development organization.

- Use your vote.

- Write to or visit elected representatives in local or national government about a particular environmental issue.

- Subscribe to an environmental pressure group, or support a conservation organization.

- Get involved in a campaigning organization.

- Get involved in non-violent direct action.

- Join a political party, or stand for election.

Some of these require little outlay of time and energy and are things we could all usefully do. Some pertain to our responsibilities as citizens in democratic countries. To use our vote effectively, we need to be aware of the policies of each party concerned. To do only this, however, can lead to a consumerist attitude to politics; we start to look to politicians to deliver a shopping list of items, but we need to know not only about their policies, but about their abilities and the extent to which we share their values. It is possible to get a much better feel for these by having some contact with them through, say, writing to them or meeting them personally to talk about a particular issue. They do tend to take notice of the size of their postbags and the people they meet face to face.

However, there can be problems and pitfalls in engaging in positive action in the world, especially those forms of action that require a greater commitment of time and effort. Burnout is common. People throw themselves into action, but after a time they find themselves unable to sustain their level of activity. In some cases, they quickly go from intense activity to complete disengagement and may end up disillusioned or cynical. Perhaps they have had an unrealistic expectation about their ability to change the world, or they've neglected their own emotional needs. Whatever the cause, we can infer that political activism cannot itself guarantee personal fulfilment.

We may find that our motivations for political activity are not what we think they are. The psychoanalyst Andrew Samuels has studied the psychological roots of political attitudes.[30] He found that the inner conflicts of his patients were frequently expressed in terms of political or environmental concern. One Italian patient, for example, expressed inner conflict in terms of anxiety about the pollution of the Adriatic coast. Similarly, our attitude to authority appears to be shaped by our relationship with our parents. There is an abundance of psychological theories on such matters, which are no doubt the subject of contention, but we have only to look at the place of nature in poetry and art to see that our minds naturally make correspondences between our inner and outer worlds. Our feelings about one get mixed up with our feelings about the other. This does not invalidate our environmental concerns – pollution, after all, does exist – but the emotional weight that we give to them may be less rational than we would like to acknowledge. So once we get involved in the thick of the action, our personal anxieties and antipathies may come to the fore.

Of course, the same goes for other people, and this raises the issue of how to work with others as part of a group or organization. Some organizations may be based in openness, self-awareness, and ethical values. Even in the environmental movement, though, this is not always the case and, at worst, groups may be dominated by desires for control, recognition, hero status, hatred for authority, or by a rigid adherence to particular views or ideologies. Pressure to conform can be subtle but strong. The environmental movement is not, to borrow a term from analytical psychology, without its shadow. Andrew Samuels refers to a 'deeply buried misanthropy', which can manifest as authoritarianism and a tendency to downgrade humanity to the level of fauna.[31] One could add to this the strong expressions of hatred and violence that emanate from some environmentalist groups.

We are likely to face difficult dilemmas. Breaking the law, for example, may appear justifiable in some cases – but how do we balance this against the long-term effects of undermining stability and social order? The more we have the personal qualities and principles that will help us deal with these pitfalls and dilemmas, the more effective we will be in the world. In particular, we need to cultivate clarity and a degree of freedom from anxiety, and we need to be firm about non-hatred.

Clarity

If we are to sustain a level of effective activity, we will need clarity and awareness of our own motivations, an ability to understand those of other people, and a strong sense of our own positive values. We should not underestimate the difficulty of achieving these and maintaining them. We can start out with the best of intentions, but it is all too easy to lose sight of our ideals. We will need to balance external activity with a degree of reflection.

This is a question not just of mental clarity but of emotional clarity as well. It implies a degree of honest self-knowledge. For example, you might find yourself holding strongly to one side or another of an argument – say, whether a particular building project is good or bad for the environment. It might be that you hold to your opinion because that's the way you've argued in the past and you fear that people won't respect you if you change your mind. It might be that you stick to one viewpoint because that's the view of your friends or your employer and you don't want to risk disapproval. Or maybe you just dislike one of the parties concerned and you have jumped to the opposite point of view out of contrariness. How much are our opinions really objective and how much are they driven by our emotions?

We also need clarity to understand how other people's actions are motivated. Why, for example, does a particular newspaper give little or no coverage to the effects of car emissions? Who owns the newspaper? What other financial interests do they have? What influence do advertisers exert over editorial content? Or, to take another example, why might scientist X give a particular opinion about global warming? Who is paying their research costs? Of course, we need to avoid a blanket cynicism that would close us off from other points of view. But, especially in a time when we are bombarded with a vast amount of information and counter-information, we need to develop a certain hard-nosed critical awareness of where it has come from.

Freedom from Anxiety

Anxiety is self-defeating and contagious. Gloominess is depressing to be around. They both get in the way of what needs to be done. You may have been in a conversation or in a meeting where this has happened. People talk incessantly about a particular issue, examining it from every viewpoint, going repeatedly over the same ground. The only thing that isn't talked about is a solution, and everyone comes away not quite sure why they're feeling mildly depressed.

Another kind of anxiety is the desire for recognition, status, or a role in society. There is the anxiety to please of the up-and-coming politician who has adopted green issues to capture the youth vote, or of the protester who goes to great lengths to get publicity and hero-status. There are also less extreme forms, of course, such as simply wanting people to congratulate you for action you've taken, or wanting to be identified by others with the environmentalist cause. To the extent that we do this, we are helping neither the world nor ourselves. Most of us, I think, experience this to some extent or other. Probably the best way of dealing with it is to be honest about it and try to let go of it as we go along.

Take some time out to reflect on your activities.

What do I hope to achieve through them? What would I like to happen within the next year, or five years?

Is this a realistic hope?

Do I tend to hold very strongly to one side of an argument? If so, why?

In what ways do I expect recognition? Does recognition make any difference to the achievement of my goals?

Dealing with Anger and Hatred

This is a very live issue in environmental activism. Is there really a problem with hatred and anger if they give us the energy to confront the causes of the problem? Is this not better than dozing in our armchairs or privately becoming hot under the collar? Firstly, we can make a useful distinction between hatred on the one hand and anger on the other.[32] An expression of anger can be simply a sudden release of frustrated energy. But even if it is not meant to harm anyone, it can be unpleasant to be on the receiving end and we need to learn to control it. This might involve the following:

- Learn to speak your mind clearly, in an appropriate way at the appropriate time.

By doing so, you are preventing the energy from becoming frustrated in the first place. It might help to rehearse beforehand what you're going to say.

- Understand what holds you back from speaking your mind on environmental issues – lack of confidence, laziness, or feelings of powerlessness?

- Don't deny your anger, but look for what's positive underneath it, such as a desire that people have more respect the environment.

- Think through the consequences of expressing anger – is it actually going to make things better, or just alienate people?

- Pause before speaking, and take a deep breath.

- Appreciate that there are limits to how much one can improve the world – it is never going to be perfect.

Realistically, this may take some time. In the meantime, a reasonably careful expression of anger might be preferable to seething with rage or the repression of one's emotions to the point of dull quiescence.

Hatred, on the other hand, is a vindictive desire for someone else's suffering. It may arise from an unacknowledged sense of personal inadequacy, or the fear of what other people think of us, or from a failure to take responsibility for our own plight. In Buddhism, it is regarded as the worst state of mind we can get ourselves into because it isolates us from others and is unpleasant or even hellish to experience. Nothing diminishes us so much as hatred.

The most direct way of defusing hatred is to use the imagination to understand and appreciate the other person as a human being. You can put yourself in the shoes of the politician, or head of a multinational corporation, or whoever is the object of your hatred, and imagine their background, their history, and all the things that have made them what they are. The more that we can do this, the more our energy can be directed not against the person but against the values and assumptions they represent. This exercise is one of the things we do in meditation, which I will say more about in the next chapter.

It might also help to recall a time in your own past when you have acted out of a similar ignorance or selfishness. What was it that changed you – was it that people expressed hatred towards you, or was it that someone communicated with you as one human being to another? This can remind us that people can change, and that, in the Buddha's own words, hatred is not stilled by hatred.

The environmental movement has given rise to collective expressions of both anger and hatred. The anti-capitalist demonstrations that accompanied recent Economic Summits are a case in point. They express understandable anger and frustration with government inaction, but they have also spilled over into hatred and violence. Anger and hatred can be distinguished in theory, but in practice it can be difficult enough even as an individual to prevent one giving rise to the other. It is more difficult still with a crowd of many thousands of people. If we get into such situations, we need to keep a clear head and make our own decisions.

If our motivation for environmental action is an attitude of non-violence, then this can only be undermined by physical or verbal violence. Perhaps most significantly, violence simply won't work as a political strategy. The success of environmentalism will depend on the creation of a broad consensus within peaceful societies. The majority of people will not look to the environmental movement for leadership if they get the impression that it is motivated by hatred. It is all too apparent to most people from recent history that political movements motivated by hatred, if successful, turn into authoritarian and repressive regimes. Hatred is ugly – it repels the very people that environmentalists need to convince.

Positive Action in Practice

If we are to exemplify these qualities of non-violence, clarity, and freedom from anxiety, our activity in the world needs to be rooted in reflection and self-knowledge. We need to make the space to ask ourselves what we're doing and why we're doing it. To be most effective, our activities will arise from the cultivation of qualities of kindness and calm and will be another expression of an ever-broadening concern for the world. In other words, it will be an integral part of the awakening of our heart and mind.

Whatever action in the world you might be engaged in, you can think about it in this light. In the next few sections I suggest some reflections that might help you to do this.

Think about the overall balance between external activity and personal cultivation in your life. Where do you fit on a spectrum between the quietist and the hyperactivist? Do you have a mixture of them both? Here are some symptoms of both ends of the spectrum, together with some signs of a more balanced approach. You could no doubt add a few of your own.

Symptoms of the quietist: Belief that I can make no difference to the world's state of affairs. I tell myself that there has always been suffering in the world, so there's no point in trying to help. Acceptance when people say that change isn't realistic. I hold back my efforts in the hope that other people or agencies will sort things out. I think a lot about imaginary utopias, what things could be like if we could only turn back the clock of technological change.

Symptoms of the hyperactivist: Fantasies about saving the environment single-handedly. Thoughts that political changes can be permanent and absolute. Expectation that political activity will make the world a perfect place. Seeing things in black and white, 'them and us'. Dogmatically lecturing to people. Making people around me more anxious when talking about environmental issues. Physical stress. Frequent conflict. Finding that my own happiness depends strongly on the success of my efforts to change things.

Signs of a balanced approach: Clarity about what I want to achieve and why. Talking to friends who understand what I am doing and why. Friendliness when engaged in activity. Openness to different ideas. Clarity about how much time and energy I am willing to spend in my activities. Ability to say no when people ask me to do things. Taking time to appreciate natural beauty and the arts.

Here is an experiment especially for hyperactivists, though of course everyone is allowed to do it. Even if you only do it once, try to put some time aside for the following exercise. Afterwards, ask yourself whether you feel any benefit. If you found the exercise difficult, ask yourself what it was that got in the way.

An Exercise for Hyperactivists

Find somewhere quiet where you can sit comfortably without being disturbed. Choose somewhere away from your everyday distractions and demands, perhaps a garden or a park. Be still for a few minutes, resisting any urge to fidget. Let the noise of your daily life fade into the background. Let go of any trains of thought. Let echoes of conversations recede. You are making silence to listen to yourself. This time is just for you.

Gently close your eyes and become aware of the sounds around you. Take an interest in them. Try to listen to them just as sounds, as if they were music. Notice any smells of the place, the feel of the air against your skin.

Open your eyes. Imagine you are seeing the world completely afresh. Instead of seeing things, try to look at shapes and colours just as shapes and colours. Imagine you're an artist about to paint the scene; where would you start?

Now become aware of your body. Feel the effect of gravity rooting you to that place – the earth pulling you down. Feel your body lifting up from the earth – your freedom to extend into the sky. Listen to the rhythm of your breathing – feel the fluidity of the air touching the solidity of your body.

In the centre of all of this, there is consciousness, there are thoughts, there are feelings. Where in your body do you experience them? Be aware of their tone. Be aware how they change from moment to moment, minute to minute.

Bring to mind other people, one by one and then more and more: all those different bodies in different places, with different thoughts and feelings.

Now come back to where you are, your own body, and the rhythm of your own breathing. After a few more minutes, gently turn your mind to whatever you are about to do next. Carry any sense of space and stillness with you as you go.

Here are a couple of exercises for quietists, just in case you were thinking there was nothing you could do.

Bring to mind someone you respect or admire who has changed the world for the better. Think about their life (read their biography, perhaps), about how insuperable the odds against them might have seemed at times. Make a list of the personal qualities that helped them to change things.

Start with one small practical thing that you adopt – for example, getting better recycling facilities in your neighbourhood. Imagine how this person might have tackled it and try to bring similar qualities to bear.

In the next few sections, I'll look at some specific areas of activity and issues that might arise in relation to them.

Political Activity

Here are some questions to think about if you are thinking about joining a political group or organization:

- Is it open to different points of view? Is there openness to free debate, or an expectation to conform?

- Does an atmosphere of anger or hatred dominate it?

- Does the group seek confrontation for its own sake?

If you are thinking of taking part in protests or demonstrations, you could ask yourself whether they are likely to be disciplined and peaceful. The New Economics Foundation Code of Protest on peaceful demonstration,[33] below, gives some very good guidelines.

NEW ECONOMICS FOUNDATION CODE OF PROTEST

We recognize that violence, in the form of poverty and exclusion, the denial of human rights and environmental destruction, is a daily experience for millions of people around the world that are losing out from globalization.

To resist and counter this, we assert our democratic rights of free speech and free assembly, to express opposition, to challenge the dominant economic orthodoxy, to promote peace and to create alternative futures. These are freedoms that are routinely and increasingly denied across the world.

Nevertheless, so that our actions are consistent with our dreams, we choose to exercise these rights in the context of the following commitments:

setting our actions within a framework of non-violence at all times,

making available at any event, campaign actions, guidance or training for non-violent protest and the defusing of violence by others,

using non-violent language, taking ownership for what we say in public and not aiming to inflame situations of protest or demonstration,

remaining curious about perspectives other than our own, recognizing that truth is our greatest asset,

focusing as far as possible on creative action, showing what we are for as well as what we protest against.

Working in the Environmental Field

Much of what has been said above will also be relevant to those employed in environmental or development organizations. These can be an excellent context for 'right livelihood' – making one's living through ethical action – the benefits of which were highly regarded by the Buddha himself. But not everything in these fields is necessarily ethical; environmental experts might, for example, be called upon to justify or mitigate the effects of a harmful development proposal. Here are some more suggested questions for those making a living through environmental action.

- Am I able to be truthful and straightforward?

- Do I ever feel pressure to be selective of the facts or slant my conclusions in a particular direction?

- Does my employer respect my integrity and independence?

- Do I stay aware of the bigger picture – the context in which my work is taking place?

- Do my colleagues and my employer share my ideals or are they as effective as I would like them to be? If not, how do I deal with this?

Environmental Education

Imparting knowledge about the environment to others, particularly children, calls for consistent clarity and inspiration. It is easy to pass on despair unconsciously, and an undervaluation of the human condition, so it is as well that educators have thought their own values through for themselves. The following suggested questions for those in environmental education may also be of interest to those who bring up children:

- Do I demonstrate clearly that actions have consequences?

- Do I encourage empathy with animals?

- How do I encourage appreciation of natural beauty?

- How do I engage children's imaginations – could I make use of story telling, art, etc?

- How can I involve children in positive action, such as conservation work and tree planting?

Activism as Self-Transformation

It might be apparent from these reflections that the balance we are trying to strike between inner reflection and outer action is not just a way of recharging our batteries. When the two are in balance, we can bring a deeper awareness to our actions. In our activity, we are putting ourselves in situations that test our qualities of clarity and kindness. In our reflection, we have the space to learn from those tests and think more deeply and creatively about what we are doing. In combination, activity and calm become in themselves a way of developing and awakening.

It is this that will be the most distinctive characteristic of Buddhist environmental activism. Self-development will always be at the forefront. This may sound curiously selfish, but it's actually quite the opposite. When the young Siddhartha, the Buddha-to-be, saw the world's suffering for the first time, he allowed it to completely transform him. He made no token gestures, turned no blind eye, and did not rest until he had given his whole being over to the deepest possible response to suffering. His emphasis on self-transformation had nothing to do with apathy or narcissism, but arose from the wholeheartedness of his search for an end to suffering.

Some implications of the centrality of self-development underlie four very useful guidelines for those involved in trying to change the world. They have been suggested by Sangharakshita in his book *What is the Sangha?*[34] I summarize them here:

- Make sure that self-development comes first. If you're not trying to change yourself, you're not going to make a truly positive contribution to anything or anyone else.

- Be in regular, personal contact with like-minded individuals.

- Withdraw support from groups or agencies that directly or indirectly discourage self-development.

- In the groups one does belong to, promote individual development by, for example, encouraging people to think for themselves.

Sustainable Activism

Changing the world is one of those things, like making friends or doing stand-up comedy, in which if you try too hard, you've blown it. It is an art for which one needs to cultivate two different but complementary qualities: forbearance and energy. Forbearance, even of a less-than-sublime nature, is an antidote to both hatred and dejection. You could, for example, reflect on the fact that life is short, perhaps shorter than you think, in relation to the timescales involved in removing the causes of the environmental crisis. You might entertain at the back of your mind the idea that you will live to see the day when humanity will live completely in harmony with nature, when all exploitation and pollution have been expunged permanently from the earth in a great triumph of environmentalism. Is this really going to happen? We will no doubt end our lives still with cause for concern about the state of the planet. We must ask ourselves, however, whether we will have forgotten to make the most of the very life that the planet has given us. Will we have been so wrapped up in busyness or hatred that we missed the chance to make a deeper and more joyful connection with other people and the beauty of nature? But the danger of becoming too forbearing is that we cease to do anything at all, so we also need to cultivate energy and an appropriate sense of the urgency of the situation. We have been born at a time when humanity faces a stark choice between learning how to share a small planet or disaster. Our lives are a precious opportunity to influence that choice for the better.

To cultivate forbearance and energy, we need both inward reflection and outward action. Action in the world, rooted in this process of awakening the heart and mind, will be neither quietist nor hyperactive. It will be a process of learning how to see that there is more suffering in the world than we can hope to address in any imaginable timescale, but not being daunted from making a start. We will need to accept that the positive changes we achieve in the world can always be reversed, but not let that deter us, and accept our own responsibility for environmental problems – not just point a finger at others.

What this adds up to is a clear sense of purpose that guides our actions from day to day and from year to year. It will consist of a continuous awareness of what we're doing and why we're doing it. We can cultivate this awareness most effectively through the practice of meditation, the subject of the next chapter.

It is with this undistracted sense of purpose, a blend of forbearance and energy, that we can most transform ourselves and the world. The more we cultivate it, the more our inner lives and their outward expression cease to compete for our time, and sustain each other. They will become, in the words of the great Zen master Hakuin, like the two wings of a bird.[35]

six

THE STILL POINT OF THE TURNING WORLD

Most of us find that our clarity – about what we are doing in our lives and why – comes and goes.[36] At some times we feel inspired and purposeful, while at others it feels as though we're just going through the motions. Things seem to get in the way and our energy doesn't flow as naturally. We don't have the same clarity all the time. We might also observe that some people seem, in general, to have more clarity than others. Obviously, clarity is not a constant. Like everything else, it fluctuates with the conditions that bring it about. The same might be said for other personal qualities, such as calm, creativity, or the degree to which we are concerned with other people. Sometimes, of course, these are conditioned by deeply ingrained psychological factors but, even then, they are not beyond the possibility of change. With effort, we can cultivate different qualities, just as we can learn to ride a bicycle or play the violin.

It follows that the degree of our environmental concern is not a constant either. It is an amalgam of different qualities, each of which can be cultivated. So what is environmental concern made of? As we have seen, it might include some anxiety and hatred among its ingredients, but we will also find positive qualities – those that will make our environmental concern more sustainable, effective, and inspiring to others – such as clarity and kindness.

We can cultivate these to some extent by consciously practising them. But a far more effective means is to combine this with the practice of meditation. It is for this reason that meditation is one of the greatest gifts that Buddhism can give to the environmental movement. Far from being a selfish escape from the troubles of the world, meditation is the very ground where we can cultivate the means of ending them. It is the crucible in which we can cultivate the qualities of generosity, ethical conduct, simplicity, forbearance, and energy. It is the heart and mind awakening itself.

There are two basic meditation practices that focus respectively on the heart and the mind. One is called the Metta Bhavana and the other the Mindfulness of Breathing. *Metta Bhavana* means the cultivation of universal loving-kindness, while the purpose of the second is to develop awareness and clarity. I am not going to give a description of the practices here – they need more space to do them justice and it is, in any case, more effective to learn them at first hand from a meditation teacher if your circumstances allow. You can contact your local Buddhist centre to find out about meditation classes[37] or read a book about these meditations.[38] I will, however, say more about why meditation is such a precious gift.

Clarity of Mind

A sustained practice of meditation helps to develop clarity and a natural ability to concentrate on something without having to force our attention on it as if holding it by the scruff of the neck. It unifies scattered energies. The kind of clarity it develops is not just clarity in the head, but a much broader awareness that encompasses the body and the emotions as well. It affects the whole self – how one is, as well as what one does. The more we meditate, the more we will communicate positive values and states of mind across a broad spectrum, with every gesture and action.

Clarity of mind also sustains awareness of others and of our effect on them. If we are really going to connect with other people, we need the clarity to identify with them imaginatively, rather than on the basis of our own feelings and prejudices. We also need clarity of mind to be watchful of our own actions – on the simplest level – to remember, for example, to turn off lights to save electricity. And clarity is essential to an effective engagement in the world because it leads to a depth of understanding and a wholeness of communication.

Kindness

Meditation helps us to develop more emotional positivity, which in turn leads to greater clarity of mind. Its effect is gradually to broaden our sphere of friendliness, kindness, and concern. Beginning with the kindness felt to our friends and ourselves, we can identify imaginatively with increasing numbers of people, with animals, and all forms of life. What grows through this identification is a genuinely other-centred concern for the world, unalloyed by our personal anxieties or dislikes. It will not be self-conscious, sugar-coated sentimentality, but real and practical.

In time, this can develop into the global sphere of concern referred to in chapter four. Our actions can be informed by a natural and heartfelt desire for the welfare of all forms of life. Specifically, we can use meditation to bring to our minds the people and animals of the future.

Breaking through Barriers

To keep up a meditation practice is not an easy option. To sit in stillness with only the workings of our own minds can be much more difficult than to lose ourselves in our daily affairs. We will come face to face with our own distraction, anxieties, laziness, petty hatred, and selfish desires. We will need all the perseverance and imagination at our disposal. One of the secrets of meditation is to turn to face the very things that get in the way of a calm and undistracted experience. These are traditionally listed as desire for sense experience, ill will, restlessness and anxiety, sloth and torpor, and doubt and indecision.

There is a clear correspondence between the barriers to meditation and the barriers to the ability to deal with the environmental crisis. Whatever estranges us from meditation estranges us from life. In turning to face the hindrances to meditation, we are also turning to face the hindrances to progress towards a safer planet. For example, we counter the desire for sense experience by cultivating contentment with the simple pleasure of meditation. Contentment and simplicity are also antidotes to the acquisitiveness and materialism that fuel exploitation and degradation.

To counter ill will, we cultivate kindness and an ability to understand the person concerned more objectively. These same qualities will help us avoid the fruitless, polarized arguments that merely add to the impasse of the environmental crisis.

To counter restlessness and anxiety, we cultivate stillness and calm. These can begin to dissolve the paralysis of fear and despair that holds many people back from effective engagement.

To deal with sloth and torpor, we try to wake ourselves up and become alert to the fact that life is short and the opportunity to meditate is precious. This same presence of mind motivates us to wake up to the urgency of the situation.

Finally, we can overcome doubt about the efficacy of meditation and our own indecision as to whether to engage with it through clear reflection on how it has worked in our previous experience. This clear reflection will help to cut through the conflicting theories and approaches to the crisis.

The personal benefits of meditation are limitless – calmness, clarity, open-heartedness, creativity, contentment, refreshment. But the benefits are not just ours. By cultivating these qualities we are not only making ourselves more happy, we are also bringing into the world the qualities that it most needs if it is to survive its current predicament.

Meditation and Evolution: An Exercise

This is an exercise that might help you think of meditation in the context of natural evolution, seeing the awakening of heart and mind as a continuation of the gradual awakening of consciousness. In meditation, we begin by developing a basis of kindly awareness of our body, mind, and emotions. We can also be developing a kindly awareness of the whole of nature. The following reflection, which is just a preliminary exercise to the meditation practices referred to above, might give a taster of this.

Sitting or lying somewhere quiet become aware of the feel of your body, from head to toe. In developing awareness of your backbone, reflect that it dates from the time when small invertebrates, floating in the sea, evolved into fish. Becoming aware of your forearms, reflect that they were developed by the amphibians that first crawled on to dry land. Your hair and warm-bloodedness came from small, early mammals to give them their own energy source and faster movement. Your long arms and strong grip came from our ape ancestors swinging through trees. And your upright posture and large skull came from the first human beings, as they used tools and developed speech. Take your time on each stage, feeling as our ancestors felt.

Remaining aware of the body, turn your attention to your feelings and emotions. It may be that they are clearly identifiable as happiness, boredom, irritation, anxiety, or it may be that you have more of a mixed soup of emotions. It might help to ask yourself where in the body you are feeling the emotions, or whether they are generally light and expansive, or heavy and contracted. You could try to imagine what colour they would be if you could see them. You can reflect that these emotions are part of being human. If you are experiencing a lot of sexual energy, you can reflect that this has come about through hundreds of millions of years of natural selection. Anxiety and hatred came about because of the instinct to survive. The point is neither to indulge your emotions, nor to be judgemental of them – just be aware what they feel like.

Having a foundation of awareness of your body and emotions, you can now take stock of your mental activity. Your mind might be sluggish or excitable, rehearsing plans for the future, re-running past conversations, or criticizing your own behaviour. You might notice that they are closely linked to your emotions and, through them, to your animal origins. You may notice that you are thinking in language, which evolved as another survival mechanism. Don't try to stop your thoughts, or become too caught up with them.

From this state of awareness, reflect that you have a choice. As an individual, you have a choice whether to act from negative, selfish impulses or from positive, expansive ones. As a species, this same choice could make the difference between extinction and survival. In our immediate experience, we carry around with us the felt memory of our evolutionary past, of our long journey from the warm seas of the young earth. We have an innate awareness of who we are and where we have come from, not only as individuals but as a species. By bringing this to mind, you are standing, as it were, at the high point of the evolutionary path that has been pioneered by our ancestors. But the point of standing here is not just to enjoy the view, but to turn and take a step further. Both for our own liberation, and to give life on earth a chance to survive, we now need to cultivate the qualities that will awaken our hearts and minds to new levels of awareness. The time has come to meditate!

seven

BEAUTY WILL SAVE THE WORLD

In September 1915, the philosopher Albert Schweitzer was travelling on a steamer along the Ogooué River in French Equatorial Africa (now Gabon).[39] He was turning over in his mind the question of what might be the soundest basis for ethics. Just then, the boat passed close to a herd of hippopotamuses. As he paused to watch them, a phrase flashed into his mind that was to become the basis of all of his future work: 'reverence for life'. This phrase came to him quite unexpectedly and unsought. It was not so much a logical deduction as a leap of intuition, a heartfelt conviction that arose in response to the beauty around him.[40]

We all have some experience of natural beauty – perhaps a passing sense of being stirred by a particular sight, or an unexpected peace and oneness with nature while out walking in the countryside. Sometimes these experiences can have a deeper feel to them, as if they concern the meaning and purpose of life itself, as if they are showing us something of how to live our lives. If, like Schweitzer, we are able to learn from them, our lives will naturally be richer and more purposeful. We will live not on the basis of moral codes or assumed ideologies, but from a heartfelt experience of truth. Natural beauty, it seems, can be a gateway to wisdom.

But how can we learn for ourselves from such experiences? We can't seek the unsought, or even expect something unexpected. We can, however, be open to the experience of beauty. We can learn to see nature with a warm heart. We can spend more time with nature. And we can reflect on it. I'll say more about each of these in the following paragraphs.

Being Open

We need to be open in a number of different ways. We need to be open-minded enough to see the world not only through facts and figures, and to recognize that we don't have all the answers. And we need to be open-hearted enough to want to seek – even long for – higher levels of truth and value. (In Buddhism, the word 'faith' denotes exactly such openness and longing, rather than referring to any sort of intellectual belief.)

We also need to be open-handed, because beauty will resist any attempt at appropriation. The truth of this struck me a few years ago. As I was setting off for a week in Scotland, a friend of mine, whose writing workshops I had been attending, set me an exercise. He suggested I write a poem about the loch in front of the retreat centre where I was staying. When I arrived, I looked and looked at the loch, but all I could see was an expanse of water occupying the glen, nothing inspiring at all. The loch was just a loch. It was only after a few days, when I'd given up in exasperation, that I was finally able to experience something of the beauty of the surroundings and write my poem. To appreciate beauty, I first had to stop grasping after it.

Sometimes, natural beauty can be difficult to resist. The majesty of a mountainous landscape, or the night sky, is such that it resists all attempts at appropriation. Not even a Sibelius or a Van Gogh can really capture them – all they can do is try to share their own sensibility to them.

Seeing with a Warm Heart

Appreciating the beauty of nature is too important to be left entirely to artists, poets, and musicians. Appreciation means seeing the world with a warm heart, which is essential if we're going to sustain our efforts to save it. There are two things that are likely to get in the way of this kind of seeing. One is seeing the world in a utilitarian way – seeing nature just as an economic resource. The other, which as environmentalists we are likely to be more prone to, is seeing the world in a problem-oriented way. The rainforest becomes just another issue to be angry about, and the sight of a blue whale is just another occasion for anxiety.

The utilitarian view can be likened to that of a gardener who creates one big vegetable patch, cutting down hedgerows, trees, and anything else that gets in the way so as to save some money on the grocery bill. The problem-oriented gardener, on the other hand, is one who can't look out of the window without worrying about when they'll find time to mow the lawn, or remarking on how pernicious the bindweed is. For both of these types, actually working in the garden is likely to be a matter of grim necessity. But for the gardener who takes time simply to enjoy the garden for its own sake, the hours spent working will melt away unnoticed. Their warm appreciation of the richness of the soil and the unique qualities of different plants will turn their work into pleasure.

With the same warm appreciation as the happily absorbed gardener, our work in the world will be enriching and invigorating. As we have seen, we can cultivate warm appreciation of people through meditation and the practice of ethics. We also need to cultivate a warm appreciation of all of nature.

Time with Nature

In practice, this means that we need to take some time away from the usual business of life to enjoy nature. The Buddha himself did this in his own life. Much of his time was spent instructing his own followers, or in walking from village to village to share his understanding with as many people as possible. He also spent time cultivating individual friendships and urged his followers to do likewise. But at other times, he would just enjoy being alone with nature.

On one occasion, feeling hemmed in by the crowds of followers, kings, ministers, and other visitors, the Buddha took off alone to spend some time in a forest. Once there, he came upon a great bull elephant, who, also feeling hemmed in by his herd, had left to find some solitude. It seems that the two recognized in each other a kindred spirit. And so, for a few months, they lived, of one mind, each delighting in the unclouded waters and tranquil solitude of the forest.[41]

Reflecting on Nature

We can get a little closer to the truths of nature through active reflection. This won't, of course, be just an intellectual exercise, but will involve feeling the truth as well as thinking it. To illustrate what I mean by this, let's try to imagine what the Buddha might have been thinking and feeling in the forest.

The Buddha taught that all things are part of interdependent networks of causes and effects. When he looked at a tree, he wouldn't just have thought 'here's a tree,' or even 'here's a beautiful tree'. You can imagine that his understanding and warm appreciation would go deeper than that. He would have seen the tree as the product of conditions – the seed of another tree, the rain, the sunlight, the nutrients in the soil around the roots. When a leaf or a branch falls, it ceases to be part of what we call the tree. If a woodcutter were to come along, the tree might be turned into a pile of firewood, leaving only the stump in the ground. So 'tree' is just a label that we attach to an arbitrarily defined part of a much bigger process. It is not a separate or permanent feature of reality, but a temporary arrangement in a flow of energy and matter. From an atom's point of view, the tree is just a stage on the journey from the atmosphere, to tree, to firewood, and to ashes.

This is not to say that the Buddha would necessarily have analysed the tree in a scientific way. Perhaps these insights would have been contained within a more intuitive appreciation of the tree's beauty. Just as he felt a natural sympathy with the bull elephant, so he would have understood what united him with the tree. A tree is made up of the same air, water, and sunlight as a human body. A mango picked from its branches one day might be a part of the human body the next. People, trees, elephants, and mangoes are not ultimately separate, they are merely labels that we attach to different parts of a greater interconnected process.

If trees are not separate and permanent features of reality, then by applying similar logic we can say the same for individual atoms, for the earth as a whole, and for ourselves. Perhaps much of the anxiety that attaches to the survival of the planet arises from a reluctance to think about one's own death. Thinking about the inevitability of death forces us to question life's meaning and purpose. It forces us to look beyond what we arbitrarily label as our self towards the mystery of whatever greater process it is that unifies all life and all things. Thinking about the inevitability of the end of life on earth – whether in a hundred years or in a hundred million years – prompts us to ask the same question all the more deeply.

In looking at a garden of roses at the height of summer, or the play of light on the sandflats as the sun goes down, one might catch a glimpse of reality. Would a rose be as beautiful if it wasn't so delicate and didn't fade in the autumn? Would the light from the sun setting over the sandflats be as beautiful if it stayed the same all day and night? In experiencing their beauty, one knows that any words one might try to attach to them will pale into insignificance.

To find ultimate meaning, according to the Buddha's teachings, one needs to see this same fragile, evanescent beauty not just in roses and sunsets, but in oneself, in other people, in all living beings and, indeed, in everything. As the *Diamond Sutra* concludes:

> As stars, a fault of vision, as a lamp,
> A mock show, dew drops, or a bubble,
> A dream, a lightning flash, or cloud,
> So should one view what is conditioned.

Indra's Net

We can learn to see this beauty not only in things viewed individually, but also in reality as a whole. As nothing is fixed, it is not ultimately separate from everything else. The *Avatamsaka Sutra*, another ancient Buddhist text, illustrates this unity in diversity by means of the simile of Indra's net. Indra, the king of the gods in Indian mythology, owns a net made of strings of jewels. Each jewel perfectly reflects, and is reflected by, every other jewel. Thus each jewel shares in the existence of every other jewel yet does not lose its individual identity.

Indra's net symbolizes an aspect of beauty that has increasingly come to light through the environmental crisis. It shines through the delicate balance of ecology, the interconnectedness of all life from the coral reefs of the Pacific Ocean to the open horizons of the African savannah. This vast net of life, which contains more species than we have yet counted, is worth cherishing not just because it is useful, but because we are part of it and it is part of us. Just as we see our selfishness reflected in the despoliation of the environment, so, in its rich beauty, we see an intimation of our own potential.

Indra's net is also a symbol for the unity of humanity. Here, spread out across the surface of a living blue-green planet, we are the universe aware of itself – each person individual and unique, yet inextricably connected. We are all in the same boat. We are in the human race and the human race, in all its beautiful diversity, is in us.

It is not just a question of seeing beauty, or talking about it or writing about it. Beauty has failed if it doesn't change us. As part of the intricate, delicate web of life, forever changing beneath the blue sky, our perspective shifts. We see living things and the world as forever changing but all the more to be cherished and revered – not from an anxiety to preserve things as they are, but from simple compassion. In losing the world, we save it.

Reflection

Try this exercise somewhere in a natural landscape, perhaps one that is familiar to you or where you have spent some time.

Look all around you. Take in the shape and form of the land, its texture, the weather, the water flowing or standing on the earth's surface, the kind of vegetation, any animals you can see. Note the forms, colours, patterns of sunlight and shade.

Feel the earth beneath where you are standing or sitting. Be aware of gravity – the solid matter in your body being drawn to the greater solid matter of the earth. Reflect that the food from which your body is made comes from the earth and will return there.

Look at the rivers and streams. Their form changes only slowly, but the water that flows through them is constantly changing. Be aware of the flow of liquid through your body – through your digestive system, your bloodstream, your skin. Water comes in and goes out, just like a stream.

Reflect on the forces that brought the earth into being, the vast energy of the expanding universe. Imagine the earth coming into being, its surface solidifying into a crust. Imagine the forces that have shaped the landscape over millions of years – the movement of the earth's surface, being worn down by ice or rivers. Feel your own physical energy – your movement, the warmth of your body. Reflect that this energy has come from the same source. The same energy that you feel inside has brought into being the landscape around you.

Watch the clouds or the wind, changing from second to second. Feel the air on your skin. Feel the air entering and leaving your body, filling your lungs and sustaining your life from moment to moment.

Reflect how dependent you are on the landscape around you, on the extent to which your body has evolved to survive on the earth's surface. Try to still your mind and sit in silence, simply experiencing yourself as part of the landscape rather than as a detached observer.

eight

TOUCHING THE EARTH

Western society is at a critical point in its history. While its influence grows ever wider, the untenability of its high-consumption, high-pollution lifestyles is becoming increasingly obvious. Growing population, weapons of mass destruction, and political instability make the situation all the more serious. The spectres are gathering at the feast. A growing number of men and women have added to the calls for change. Scientists, writers, and artists have used their skills; protesters have taken to bulldozers, shovels, and inflatable dinghies; many more have dug into their pockets to support campaign organizations. Change has come about, but on nothing like the scale required to avert disaster. Something much deeper needs to turn around.

Meanwhile, the teachings of Siddhartha Gautama, the Buddha, have arrived in the West. It is gradually beginning to dawn on large numbers of people that they are not just an exotic diversion, or another eastern philosophy, or even another religion as we might understand the term.

From the accounts of his life, there shines through not an esoteric, otherworldly guru, but a vividly human figure searching for happiness, meaning, and purpose. These he found and taught to others as the path of transformation, awakening the heart and mind.

Buddhism has no bold new blueprint to offer the world. It has no ideology to hand down. There is nothing new in qualities such as generosity, empathy, or clarity of mind. What Buddhism has to offer is the perspective that, however awake we already are, we can all wake up more fully. It is a practical path of harnessing all of one's energies, one's whole being, to the process of change. It offers a means of becoming more effective in the task of motivating people to change. It is also a path to personal freedom and happiness. It is a way of changing what seems unchangeable, both in the world and in us.

A Buddhist vision of environmentalism will be firmly rooted in a conscious effort to wake up to the fact that we are connected with others and with the natural world. Through meditation and reflection, it will be based on insights that have become our own. It will be made up of ordinary, human acts of generosity. It will be a joint rather than an individual effort and will be infused with a spirit of clarity and calm.

It is in the nature of Buddhism that it freely gives away its insights and practices with open-handed generosity. We don't have to call ourselves Buddhists to meditate, practise generosity, or reflect on beauty. We don't have to wait for a large-scale conversion to Buddhism in the West for it to have a positive effect. This is just as well, since that might take too long.

Perhaps it is not so difficult to imagine that an awareness of the value of meditation, a language of ethical conduct, and simplicity of lifestyle might begin to move from the fringes to the mainstream of our culture. This could happen if, Buddhist or not, we make it happen.

In its energy and engagement with the world, the environmental movement may have something important to offer Buddhists. Looking back, it seems that the greatest social issue of the Buddha's day was the caste system. The Buddha's response to this was clear, uncompromising, and vocal. For himself, he rejected all the badges and privileges of his caste. In his interactions, he confounded the expectations of others by befriending outcastes and exposing the assumptions of those of high caste. Among his disciples, from the very outset, he would allow no such distinctions to be made. His whole being – body, speech, and mind – reflected his rejection of the dehumanization of caste. With unbounded clarity and kindness, he challenged and exposed the suppositions and prejudices that underpinned the injustices of his day.

On the path of awakening the heart and mind, should we be any less clear, uncompromising, or vocal about the suppositions and prejudices that underpin the injustices of our own time?

When the Buddha, at the moment of his awakening, lightly touched the earth, it was recognition, a remembrance, of where he had come from and what he had attained. But that touch also contained a promise – the promise of transformation. When an awakening heart and mind touches the world, the result is change. Today, as the Buddha is no longer here, that is up to us.

RECOMMENDED READING

General Buddhism
Ayya Khema, *Being Nobody Going Nowhere: Meditations on the Buddhist Path*, Wisdom: Boston, Mass. 1987
Tejananda, *The Buddhist Path to Awakening*, Windhorse: Birmingham 1999

Ethics
Marshall B. Rosenberg, *Nonviolent Communication: A Language of Compassion*, Puddledancer: Encinitas, Calif. 1999
Sangharakshita, *The Ten Pillars of Buddhism*, Windhorse: Birmingham 1996

Meditation
Paramananda, *Change Your Mind: A Practical Guide to Buddhist Meditation*, Windhorse: Birmingham 1996

Buddhism, the Environment, and Politics
David Edwards, *The Compassionate Revolution: Radical Politics and Buddhism*, Green: Totnes 1998

Joanna Macy, *World as Lover, World as Self*, Parallax: Berkeley, Calif. 1991

Reflections and Exercises

Wes Nisker, *Buddha's Nature: Who We Really Are and Why This Matters*, Rider: London 1998

Paramananda, *A Deeper Beauty: Buddhist Reflections on Everyday Life* Windhorse: Birmingham 2001

John Seed, Joanna Macy, Pat Fleming, and Arne Naess, *Thinking Like a Mountain: Towards a Council of All Beings*, New Society: Gabriola Island, Canada 1988

A Short Novel

Jean Giono, *The Man Who Planted Trees*, Harvill: London 1995

Some Useful Websites

There are several websites mentioned in this book and in the notes and references. Here are some more:

To calculate the amount of carbon emissions you are responsible for, visit www.carboncalculator.org or www.co2.org

To contact a group of environmentally engaged Buddhists active within the Friends of the Western Buddhist Order, go to www.ecopractice.fwbo.org

NOTES AND REFERENCES

1   *Ratnaguna-Samcayagatha Sutra*

2   Tubwebwe features in a book by Tony Wheeler and Peter Bennetts, *Lonely Planet: Time and Tide – The Islands of Tuvalu*, Lonely Planet: 2001.

3   Honufa tells more of her story on the Water Aid website: www.wateraid.org.uk

4   Presentation by Robert T. Watson, Chair of the Intergovernmental Panel on Climate Change, to the Sixth Conference of Parties to the United Nations Framework Convention on Climate Change, 13 November 2000

5   Simon Stuart, *Species: Unprecedented Extinction Rate, And It's Increasing*, IUCN, the World Conservation Union; *Endangered Species of the Next Millennium*, IUCN press release, originally published online in 1999 at www.iucn. org. Currently archived at envirodebate.org

6   Jonathon Porritt, *Save the Earth*, Dorling Kindersley: 1992

7   Karl Marx, 'Theses on Feuerbach' in Friedrich Engels, Karl Marx, *The German Ideology: Including Thesis on Feuerbach*, Prometheus: 1998

8   For a much fuller exploration of this topic, see Robin Cooper (Ratnaprabha), *The Evolving Mind: Buddhism, Biology, and Consciousness*, Windhorse: Birmingham 1996.

9   See Christopher S. Queen and Sallie B. King (eds.) *Engaged Buddhism: Buddhist Liberation Movements in India*, State University of New York Press: Albany 1996, pp. 17 ff.

10 Tom Athanasiou, *Divided Planet: The Ecology of Rich and Poor*, Little, Brown: New York 1996

11 An unnamed former director of Greenpeace, quoted in Tom Athanasiou, *Slow Reckoning: The Ecology of a Divided Planet*, Secker & Warburg: London 1997

12 For more details on these 'six perfections' see Sangharakshita, *A Survey of Buddhism*, 9th edition, Windhorse: Birmingham 2001, pp. 466 ff.

13 The chapter title is the epigraph in E.M. Forster's novel, *Howards End*.

14 Helena Norberg-Hodge, *Ancient Futures: Learning from Ladakh*, Rider: London 1992

15 Thich Nhat Hanh, *Being Peace*, Parallax: Berkeley 1987, pp. 11–12

16 André Gorz, *Capitalism, Socialism, Ecology*, trans. Chris Turner, Verso: London 1994, p. 4

17 Tor Nørretranders, *The User Illusion: Cutting Consciousness Down To Size*, Penguin: London 1999

18 There is a growing amount of work to replace the Gross National Product, which only measures financial transactions, with a measure that takes account of social,

cultural, and environmental factors. The Government of Bhutan, for example, has introduced a measure of Gross National Happiness. See Sander G. Tideman, *Gross National Happiness: Towards Buddhist Economics*, 2001, available online through the New Economics Foundation at www.neweconomics.org

19 See www.idealist.org for a wide range of international volunteering opportunities.

20 For information on becoming a conservation volunteer in the UK, contact the BTCV at www.btcv.org.uk 01491 821600.

21 For information on LETS schemes in the UK and elsewhere, see www.letslinkuk.org

22 *Culagosinga Sutta*, Majjhima-Nikaya 31

23 The chapter title is taken from Henry David Thoreau: 'Our life is frittered away by detail ... Simplify, simplify.' *Walden and Civil Disobedience*, Penguin: London 1983, p.136.

24 *Kutadanta Sutta*, Digha-Nikaya 5.22 ff.

25 Intergovernmental Panel on Climate Change, *Aviation and the Global Atmosphere*, 1999

26 You can check out the implications of your own journey at www.chooseclimate.org/flying/mapcalc.html

27 Nicholas Hildyard, 'Foxes in Charge of Chickens', in Wolfgang Sachs (ed.) *Global Ecology: A New Arena of Political Conflict*, Zed: London 1993

28 Bodhipaksa, *Vegetarianism*, Windhorse: Birmingham 1999

29 Sangharakshita, from 'The Simple Life', in *Crossing the Stream*, Windhorse: Birmingham 1987

30 Andrew Samuels, *The Political Psyche*, Routledge: London 1993, p. 62

31 ibid., p. 103

32 See Sangharakshita, *Know Your Mind: The Psychological Dimension of Ethics in Buddhism*, Windhorse: Birmingham 1998, p. 164

33 For further details see the news archive at www. neweconomics.org or contact the New Economics Foundation, Cinnamon House, 6–8 Cole Street, London SE1 4YH; 020 7407 7447 or email info@neweconomics.org.

34 Sangharakshita, *What is the Sangha? The Nature of Spiritual Community*, Windhorse: Birmingham 2000, pp. 239 ff.

35 Hakuin Zenji, *Selections from the Embossed Tea Kettle*, Paul H. Crompton: 1986, p. 45

36 The chapter title is taken from T.S. Eliot's *Four Quartets.*

37 To find a Buddhist centre near you, try for example www. fwbo.org, samatha.demon.co.uk, or manjushri.org.uk; if there is no centre near you, try www.wildmind.org for online meditation teaching.

38 For example, Paramananda, *Change Your Mind: A Practical Guide to Buddhist Meditation*, Windhorse: Birmingham 1996

39 The chapter title is paraphrased from Fyodor Dostoevsky's *The Idiot.*

40 Quoted in Peter Marshall, *Nature's Web: Rethinking Our Place on Earth*, Cassell: London 1992

41 *Udana* iv.5

INDEX

The windhorse symbolizes the energy of the Enlightened mind
carrying the truth of the Buddha's teachings to all corners of the world.
On its back the windhorse bears three jewels: a brilliant gold jewel
represents the Buddha, the ideal of Enlightenment, a sparkling blue
jewel represents the teachings of the Buddha, the Dharma, and a
glowing red jewel, the community of the Buddha's enlightened
followers, the Sangha. Windhorse Publications, through the medium of
books, similarly takes these three jewels out to the world.

Windhorse Publications is a Buddhist publishing house, staffed by
practising Buddhists. We place great emphasis on producing books of
high quality, accessible and relevant to those interested in Buddhism at
whatever level. Drawing on the whole range of the Buddhist tradition,
Windhorse books include translations of traditional texts,
commentaries, books that make links with Western culture and ways
of life, biographies of Buddhists, and manuals on meditation.

As a charitable institution we welcome donations to help us continue
our work. We also welcome manuscripts on aspects of Buddhism or
meditation. For orders and catalogues contact

WINDHORSE PUBLICATIONS	WINDHORSE BOOKS	WEATHERHILL INC
11 PARK ROAD	P O BOX 574	41 MONROE TURNPIKE
BIRMINGHAM	NEWTOWN	TRUMBULL
B13 8AB	NSW 2042	CT 06611
UK	AUSTRALIA	USA

Windhorse Publications is an arm of the Friends of the Western Buddhist Order, which has more than sixty centres on five continents. Through these centres, members of the Western Buddhist Order offer regular programmes of events for the general public and for more experienced students. These include meditation classes, public talks, study on Buddhist themes and texts, and 'bodywork' classes such as t'ai chi, yoga, and massage. The FWBO also runs several retreat centres and the Karuna Trust, a fund-raising charity that supports social welfare projects in the slums and villages of India.

Many FWBO centres have residential spiritual communities and ethical businesses associated with them. Arts activities are encouraged too, as is the development of strong bonds of friendship between people who share the same ideals. In this way the FWBO is developing a unique approach to Buddhism, not simply as a set of techniques, less still as an exotic cultural interest, but as a creatively directed way of life for people living in the modern world.

If you would like more information about the FWBO visit the website at www.fwbo.org or write to

LONDON BUDDHIST CENTRE
51 ROMAN ROAD
LONDON
E2 0HU
UK

ARYALOKA
HEARTWOOD CIRCLE
NEWMARKET
NH 03857
USA

ALSO FROM WINDHORSE

PARAMANANDA

A DEEPER BEAUTY:

BUDDHIST REFLECTIONS ON EVERYDAY LIFE

In *A Deeper Beauty*, Paramananda speaks directly to our hearts about what is truly important to us. Using simple exercises, reflections, and meditations, we can awaken to the magic of being fully present in each moment of our day-to-day activities.

Paramananda draws on his experience as a hospice worker and Buddhist meditation teacher in an imaginative and a down-to-earth way, offering us courage, kindness, and joy in our search for meaning.

208 pages
ISBN 1 899579 44 3
£8.99/$16.95

BODHIPAKSA

VEGETARIANISM

Part of a series on *Living a Buddhist Life*, this book explores connections between vegetarianism and the spiritual life.

As a trained vet, Bodhipaksa is well placed to reveal the suffering of animals in the farming industry, and as a practising Buddhist he can identify the ethical consequences of inflicting such suffering. Through the Buddhist teaching of interconnectedness he lays bare the effects our eating habits can have upon us, upon animals, and upon the environment.

He concludes that by becoming vegetarian we can affirm life in a very clear and immediate way, and so experience a greater sense of contentment, harmony, and happiness.

112 pages
ISBN 1 899579 15 X
£4.99/$9.95

PARAMANANDA

CHANGE YOUR MIND:

A PRACTICAL GUIDE TO BUDDHIST MEDITATION

Buddhism is based on the truth that, with effort, we can change the way we are. But how? Among the many methods Buddhism has to offer, meditation is the most direct. It is the art of getting to know one's own mind and learning to encourage what is best in us.

   This is an approachable and thorough guide to meditation, based on traditional material but written in a light and modern style. Colourfully illustrated with anecdotes and tips from the author's experience as a meditator and teacher, it also offers refreshing inspiration to seasoned meditators.

208 pages, with photographs
ISBN 0 904766 81 0
£8.99/$17.95

JINANANDA

MEDITATING

This is a guide to Buddhist meditation that is in sympathy with a modern lifestyle. Accessible and thought-provoking, this books tells you what you need to know to get started with meditation, and to keep going through the ups and downs of everyday life. Realistic, witty, and very inspiring.

128 pages
ISBN 1 899579 07 9
£4.99/$9.95